The Civil War
1863-1865

The
MILITARY HISTORY
of the
UNITED STATES

Christopher Chant

The Civil War
1863-1865

MARSHALL CAVENDISH
NEW YORK · LONDON · TORONTO · SYDNEY

Library Edition Published 1992

© Marshall Cavendish Limited 1992

Published by
Marshall Cavendish Corporation
2415 Jerusalem Avenue
PO Box 587
North Bellmore
New York 11710

Series created by Graham Beehag Book Design

Series Editor	Maggi McCormick
Consultant Editors	James R. Arnold
	Roberta Wiener
Sub Editor	Julie Cairns
Designer	Graham Beehag
Illustrators	John Batchelor
	Steve Lucas
	Terry Forest
	Colette Brownrigg
Indexer	Mark Dartford

The publishers wish to thank the following organizations
who have supplied photographs:

The National Archives, Washington. United States
Navy, United States Marines, United States Army,
States Air Force, Department of Defense, Library of
Congress, The Smithsonian Institution.

The publishers gratefully thank the U.S. Army Military
History Institute, Carlisle Barracks, PA. for the use of
archive material for the following witness accounts:

Page 70
*A History of the Seventy-Third Regiment of Illinois
Infantry Volunteers.* (Chattanooga, 1890).

Page 74-5
*Personal Memoirs of P.H. Sheridan, General United
States Army.* (New York, 1888).

Page 130
Military Memoirs of a Confederate, by Edward P.
Alexander, (New York, 1907).

Library of Congress Cataloging-in-Publication Data

Chant, Christopher.
   The Military History of the United States / Christopher Chant –
Library ed.
      p. cm.
   Includes bibliographical references and index.
   Summary: Surveys the wars that have directly influenced the
United States., from the Revolutionary War through the Cold War.
   ISBN 1-85435-357-8 ISBN 1-85435-361-9 (set)
   1. United States - History, Military - Juvenile literature.
[1. United States - History, Military.] I. Title.
t181.C52 1991
973 - dc20   90 - 19547
                                                  CIP
                                                  AC

Printed in Singapore by Times Offset PTE Ltd
Bound in the United States

Contents

At the very beginning of 1863, the Confederacy appeared to have a better than even chance of winning the Civil War on the battlefield. However, during 1863, three major campaigns took place that dashed not only the military plans, but even the hopes of the Confederacy. The three campaigns were on the Mississippi River, where control passed finally to the Federal forces; that fought in the eastern theater during the same period, which finally ended all chances of the Confederacy invading the north and gaining a success so stunning that a major European power might be persuaded to recognize and aid the Confederacy; and in the center where Federal military success, at first uncertain and lacking in decisive speed at last gave the Union control of the starting point on the main route into the Confederacy's heartlands on the Atlantic coast.

The strategic penetration south down the Mississippi River began with Brigadier General (later Major General) Ulysses Simpson Grant's campaign to take Forts Henry and Donelson, and was then pursued in the Shiloh campaign. Federal progress then slowed once Major General Henry Wager Halleck arrived to supervise operations against Corinth, Mississippi, which fell to the Federal forces on May 30, 1862. Though Halleck launched a short-term pursuit of the Confederate forces, on June 11, he decided to halt and consolidate the Federal position in Tennessee rather than pursue the Confederate army deep into Mississippi.

Divided Command in the West

In July 1862, Halleck was recalled to Washington to take over from Major General George Brinton McClellan as general in chief of the Federal army. The army of Halleck's Department of the Mississippi was now divided between Grant (60,000 men of the Army of the Tennessee) and Major General Don Carlos Buell (56,000 men of the Army of the Ohio). Grant's main task was the

On January 1, 1863, a Confederate force under Major General John Bankhead Magruder captured the port of Galveston. With the support of two converted steamers, the *Neptune* and *Bayou City*, Magruder then attacked the Federal gunboats in the harbor. The *Harriet Lane* was taken, and after the *Westfield* had run aground, the Federal commander W.B. Renshaw ordered her set on fire. The ship blew up prematurely, and Renshaw was one of those killed. Galveston remained in Confederate hands, but under Federal blockade, until its surrender on June 2, 1865.

protection of Federal lines of communication in western Tennessee, while the role of Buell (later replaced by Major General William Starke Rosecrans in command of what had by then become the Army of the Cumberland) was the defeat of Major General Braxton Bragg's invasion of Kentucky.

In western Tennessee, Grant chafed at the inaction forced upon him, for he was fully aware of the strategic significance of dividing the Confederacy by winning control of the Mississippi River. Here the only obstacles to Federal success were the Confederate garrisons of 6,000 men at Vicksburg, Mississippi, and 5,500 men at Port Hudson, Louisiana. Naval expeditions mounted against these two garrisons from New Orleans, under the command of Captain (soon Rear Admiral) David Glasgow Farragut, were repulsed without difficulty in May and July 1862. The most northern point of Federal control was now Baton Rouge, Louisiana, where there was an 11,000-man garrison of the Department of the Gulf. In the fall of the same year, Grant pressed Halleck for permission to move onto the offensive. Finally, on October 25, Halleck signaled to Grant: "Fight the enemy where you please."

The Mississippi River: Key to the War

The Confederacy realized the importance of denying the Union full use of the Mississippi River. On October 13, Lieutenant General John Clifford Pemberton was appointed to command the Department of Mississippi, Tennessee and East Louisiana with special responsibility for the defense of Vicksburg.

Grant's first scheme was an advance by five divisions, totaling about 40,000 men, virtually due south along the line of the Mississippi Central Railroad. The Federal advance began on November 2 and at first seemed to be the correct course of action. The Confederate local commander, Major General Earl Van Dorn, had a sizeable force at his disposal, but seemed reluctant to move against Grant. As the Federal force advanced, the Confederates pulled back through north-

ern Mississippi from Holly Springs to Grenada. Grant reached Holly Springs on November 20 and four days later moved forward again. By December 5, the Federal force was 15 miles south of Oxford and well on the way to Grenada.

At this point, Confederate resistance began to appear. Van Dorn sensibly decided that his 24,000 men were inadequate for the task of a frontal assault, so he led 3,500 cavalry around Grant's left flank to strike at the Federal line of communications by recapturing Holly Springs on November 20 before pressing on toward Bolivar and then swinging back to the south. More Federal confusion was produced by another Confederate cavalry raid farther north. Here, Brigadier General Nathan Bedford Forrest's force struck Jackson, Tennessee, on December 20 and then moved north to destroy some 60 miles of railroad before swinging away to the southeast at the end of the year.

Nathan Bedford Forrest was one of the Confederacy's finest leaders of cavalry. Born in 1821 to a poor Tennessee family, Forrest had acquired considerable wealth by the time he enlisted as a private soldier just before his fortieth birthday. He then raised a mounted battalion at his own expense. The finest testimony to Forrest's success as a raider is Sherman's statement during the Atlanta campaign of 1864: "That devil Forrest hunted down and killed if it costs ten thousand lives and bankrupts the Federal treasury."

Waterborne Advance to Vicksburg

Halleck was already concerned that Grant's plan was not adequate. He suggested that a riverborne move against Vicksburg offered a greater chance of success. By December 5, Grant had reached the same conclusion and recast his offensive to include a riverborne component that turned the offensive into a two-prong advance. It is likely that just as Grant was influenced by Halleck, the general in chief had been influenced in this direction by President Abraham Lincoln.

Even as Grant was preparing to get his men onto the move, another plan had been maturing in Washington. Lincoln and Secretary of War Edwin McMasters Stanton had long appreciated the importance of the Mississippi River and had now planned an offensive to turn it into a Federal waterway. Into this situation stepped Major General John Alexander McClernand, who persuaded the president that he could raise substantial forces in the midwest, assemble them at Memphis, and then move down the Mississippi to take Vicksburg in a combined army and navy operation. McClernand was an officer of little proven ability, but was politically astute and had the ear of the administration. Lincoln latched onto McClernand's idea with enthusiasm and added his own component: a simultaneous advance from Baton Rouge, in the south, by the 11,000 men of Major General Nathaniel Prentiss Banks, another political officer who had succeeded Major General Benjamin Franklin Butler as the head of the Department of the Gulf.

Halleck knew little of this background, but when he learned of McClernand's task, which was to be an independant offensive in Grant's department, he persuaded Lincoln to make McClernand subordinate to Grant.

On December 9, Grant detached Major General William Tecumseh Sherman with the 32,000 men of four divisions to return to Memphis, Tennessee. Here the force embarked in a Federal river flotilla. It departed from Memphis on December 20,

steamed down the Mississippi River to land just north of Vicksburg, on the southern bank of the Yazoo River just upstream of its junction with the Mississippi River, during December 26. Grant planned to advance slightly more to the south and then halt in positions that would allow his force to move forward swiftly as soon as Sherman's riverborne operation began to yield results around Vicksburg.

However, the raids of Van Dorn and Forrest forced Grant to adjust his scheme. On December 21, he pulled back his remaining strength from Oxford to Grand Junction, Tennessee.

The Battle of Chickasaw Bluffs

North of Vicksburg, meanwhile, the four divisions of Sherman's XIII Corps spent

William Tecumseh Sherman was Grant's right-hand man throughout most of the Civil War, and certainly one of the outstanding generals of the conflict.

David Dixon Porter was the son of Commodore David Porter, a major figure of the War of 1812. Born in Pennsylvania in 1813, Porter joined the U.S. Navy in 1829 and was promoted to commander in April, 1861. Porter commanded the force of mortar schooners that took part in the capture of New Orleans in March 1862 under his foster brother, David Farragut. In September 1862, he took over the Mississippi Squadron with the acting rank of rear admiral and participated in several campaigns in the region. In October 1864, he was appointed commander of the North Atlantic Squadron and took part in the campaign that resulted in the Federal capture of Fort Fisher, North Carolina, between January 6 and 15, 1865. Porter was promoted to vice admiral in 1866 and to admiral of the navy in 1870. He died in 1891.

FORT FISHER

the two days after their arrival working their way through bayous and swamps to an assault position near Chickasaw Bluffs. On the day of Sherman's arrival on the Yazoo River, Pemberton had been able to reinforce the 6,000-man garrison of Vicksburg with another 7,000 men sent by rail from Jackson, Mississippi. The garrison commander, Major General Martin Luther Smith, was thus able to deploy 10,700 men in prepared positions to face the attack of the 25,000 Federal troops deployed, from right to left, in the divisions commanded by Brigadier Generals Andrew Jackson Smith, Morgan Lewis Smith, George Washington Morgan, and Frederick Steele.

The Battle of Chickasaw Bluffs on December 29, 1862, was a straightforward Union defeat that cost the Confederates only 207 casualties to the Federal force's 1,776 (208 killed, 1,005 wounded, and 563 missing). As Sherman himself put it: "I reached Vicksburg at the time appointed, landed, assaulted, and failed." Sherman then planned to move farther up the Yazoo River in an effort to strike at the Confederates' right flank, but on January 2, 1863, he abandoned this plan and fell back to the mouth of the Yazoo River. Here, McClernand was waiting to assume command of what became the Army of the Mississippi.

McClernand's Division of Effort

However, instead of resuming the attack on Vicksburg, McClernand decided to move 30,000 men in 50 transports, backed by 13 gunboats under Rear Admiral David Dixon Porter, back up the Mississippi River to attack Fort Hindman at Arkansas Post on the Arkansas River. McClernand reasoned that this was a refuge from which Confederate gunboats could harass Federal shipping on the Mississippi River. Brigadier T.J. Churchill's 5,500-man Confederate garrison surrendered on January 12, largely as a result of the naval bombardment of its positions. Confederate losses were 4,900 (including 4,791 captured) and those of McClernand's army 1,061. As soon as he heard of the operation, Grant ordered McClernand to return to Vicksburg so that his complete force would be in position to support Grant once he arrived.

Only on December 18 did Grant learn that McClernand, an officer whose capabilities he strongly distrusted, was to command the river force, since he was senior to Sherman. Coupled with the Confederate raids in his rear, this was enough to persuade Grant that any idea of an overland advance should be abandoned and his main strength be moved by river to Vicksburg. Leaving the 62,000 men of Major General Stephen Augustus Hurlbut's XVI Corps to guard the rear areas of western Tennessee and northern Mississippi, Grant embarked for Vicksburg, where he arrived on January 29 and assumed command on the following day. Grant's strength outside Vicksburg was 45,000 men of McClernand's XIII Corps, Sherman's XV Corps, and Major General James Birdseye McPherson's XVII Corps.

Vicksburg's Natural and Man-made Defenses

Vicksburg was well sited for defense. The bluffs rose to a height of 250 feet above the river and stretched about 100 miles from north to south. North of Vicksburg was the Yazoo River and its delta, an area of bayous and swampy bottom land measuring 175 miles from north to south,

and 60 miles from east to west. South of the city was a slightly smaller, but no less impenetrable, area of a similar nature. To these natural defenses, the Confederates had added man-made features in the form of fortifications stretching from Haynes Bluff, 10 miles up the Yazoo River, to Grand Gulf about 40 miles below Vicksburg on the mouth of the Big Black River. It was impossible to assault Vicksburg directly from the Mississippi River, therefore, and passage past the Confederate defenses in the city was hazardous, as the river made a U-bend that kept vessels within range of the guns for a long time.

Any attack on Vicksburg with a real chance of success had to be launched from the east, which would make the Federal force the meat in a sandwich between Pemberton's Vicksburg forces, which rose to a strength of 30,000, and the steadily growing forces being drawn together at Jackson by General Joseph Eggleston Johnston, heading the Department of the West with control over Pemberton's Army of Mississippi and Bragg's Army of Tennessee.

Winter Operations

During the winter of 1862-63, rain fell heavily and the Mississippi region became all but impassable. The rivers were in spate; the land became a muddy morass even on well-established roads. In the short term, therefore, Grant's major problems were not so much the Confederate garrison as the conditions in which his men were forced to live, and increasingly outspoken criticism by Union politicians and newspapers. In an attempt to placate his critics, Grant made five efforts to reach the high ground east of Vicksburg between February and April 1863. All five efforts were defeated by the conditions or the Confederates. It is eloquent testimony of Grant's determination that the efforts continued, and of Lincoln's faith in Grant that the efforts were allowed to continue.

The first attempt was a short canal across the neck of land opposite Vicksburg, which Sherman's troops dug from January in an effort to provide a means

William Tecumseh Sherman

For further references see pages
8, 9, 12, 13, 15, 16, 20, 21, 26, 28, 69, 70, 71, 72, 74, 80, 82, *85*, 96, 97, 101, *102*, *103*, *106*, 108, 109, 113, *116*, 117, 118, *119*, 120, 122, 123, 124, 131

Right: Monitors were shallow-draft vessels mounting one or two large-caliber guns. They were designed specifically for bombarding stationary targets such as moored ships or shore installations. Many of these steam-powered ships were built for the Federal navy during the Civil War; and seen here is the U.S.S. *Onondaga*, built by the Continental Iron Works and commissioned in March 1864. It was the navy's first double-turret monitor. Each turret accommodated one 15-inch Dahlgren rifled gun and one 150-pounder Parrott rifled gun. Power was provided by four engines delivering 420 horsepower to two propellers. The ship saw only limited action against Confederate ironclads in the James River. It was sold to France in 1867 and was a coast defense battleship until 1903.

for troop transports to pass Vicksburg without running the gauntlet of the Confederate guns. The attempt had to be abandoned on March 29 because of the high water level.

The second attempt was more ambitious. It envisaged a canal from the Mississippi River at Duckport to link up with the bayous farther from Vicksburg, west of Sherman's canal, so that steamers could pass through and then back into the Mississippi River 20 miles below Vicksburg. One steamer finally made the passage, but the scheme then had to be abandoned, ironically, because of low water levels!

The third attempt was made simultaneously with the first two and involved the troops of McPherson's corps. It was similar to the first two in being an attempt to bypass Vicksburg, but still farther to the west. It involved a 400-mile route from Lake Providence through the lakes swamps, and bayous of Louisiana to arrive back at the Mississippi River well below Vicksburg. Considerable progress was made before the attempt was abandoned at the end of March for more promising plans.

The fourth attempt involved blasting the levee on the eastern side of the Mississippi River, 325 miles north of Vicksburg, to open the Yazoo Pass and so allow Federal transports to cross eventually into the Tallahatchie River and thus into the Yazoo River. Even though it involved a 700-mile journey to get Federal troops back to Vicksburg from Miliken's Bend, the Federal base area only 30 miles upstream of Vicksburg, Grant had high hopes of the route. It allowed effective use of the Federal naval superiority and

was not susceptible to Confederate cavalry raids. It was hoped that 30,000 men could be moved onto the high ground east of Vicksburg by this route, but Pemberton appreciated the threat and sent Major General William Wing Loring's division to block the route. The division quickly built Fort Pemberton, about 90 miles north of Vicksburg, and the gunboats spearheading the Federal effort were halted on March 11; six days later, the Federal force withdrew.

The fifth attempt resulted from a reconnaissance of Steele's Bayou with a view to supporting the Yazoo Pass expedition. As the reconnaissance continued farther upstream, it became clear that Steele's Bayou, a tributary of the Yazoo River running approximately parallel to the Mississippi River, offered possibilities of its own. Porter led 11 vessels up the bayou as Sherman followed with troops on foot. The Confederates halted Porter at Rolling Fork,where his vessels could have crossed over to the Sunflower River for the trip back to a point 200 miles higher up the Yazoo River. Hearing late on March 19 that Porter had been trapped, Sherman undertook a daring night march illuminated by candles in the muzzles of his men's rifles and saved Porter.

Grant Unveils His Definitive Plan

On April 4, Grant confided to Halleck his definitive plan for the capture of Vicksburg. The plan was a very bold undertaking and relied completely on the gunboats and transports of Porter's flotilla being able to run past the Confederate guns in Vicksburg without suffering undue loss. Leaving Sherman's corps to divert the Confederates north of Vicksburg, Grant planned to move the corps of McPherson and McClernand south from Miliken's Bend on the western side of the Mississippi River to a point south of Vicksburg, where they would be ferried across the river in Porter's vessels and with only five days' rations, strike inland to arrive in the Confederates' rear. As Grant told Sherman, the Federal troops would carry "what rations of hard bread, coffee, and salt we can and make the country furnish the balance."

While McClernand was willing to undertake the plans, both Porter and Sherman tried to persuade Grant that the plan was too risky. Halleck left the decision to Grant, but reminded him of the need to aid Banks against Port Hudson before moving against Vicksburg. On April 11, Grant informed Halleck that once Porter's vessels had moved the bulk of the army across the Mississippi River, he would detach one corps to the aid of Banks. This satisfied Halleck, and Grant's offensive moved into gear.

On March 29, McClernand's corps received orders to open the way past Vicksburg on the western side of the Mississippi River. They set off on April 5. The route lay through wide bottom land, but with the aid of corduroy roads to supplement the barges and small

Henry Wager Halleck

For further references see pages 6, 7, 8, 15, 44, 58, 60, 70, 75, 78, 86, 92

of his corps south, leaving only one division and one brigade to guard the Federal base at Miliken's Bend.

Slow Confederate Response

Despite the fact that the first Federal troops departed from Miliken's Bend on April 5, it was not until April 17 that Pemberton learned of the move. By April 28, Pemberton had deduced that the first objective for any Federal activity south of Vicksburg would be Grand Gulf. He despatched 5,000 men to reinforce the 4,000 already in the area under the command of Brigadier General John S. Bowen. This still left Bowen with wholly inadequate strength to tackle the considerably larger Federal forces, but Pemberton was unable to send further reinforcement as he had already diluted his own strength. This was a result of the Grierson raid, whose size and import had been overestimated by Pemberton.

Grierson's Cavalry Raid

The raid had been planned by Grant for just this purpose. Under the command of Colonel Benjamin Henry Grierson, 1,700 cavalry supported by two 6-pounder guns left La Grange, Tennessee, on April 17 to strike through the Confederate rear areas before reaching Banks's force at Baton Rouge on May 2. In the course of 16 days, the raiders covered some 600 miles and convinced the Confederates that major events were under way in their rear. It was one of the most daring and successful cavalry raids of the war, and Grierson's own laconic report summarizes it nicely:

"During the expedition we killed and wounded about one hundred of the enemy, captured and paroled over 500 prisoners...destroyed between fifty and sixty miles of railroad and telegraph, captured and destroyed over 3,000 stand of arms, and other army stores and Government property to an immense amount; we also captured 1,000 horses and mules.

"Our loss during the entire journey was 3 killed, 7 wounded, 5 left on the route sick; the sergeant-major and surgeon of

On April 16, 1863, Porter's Mississippi Squadron managed to run 11 of its 12 main vessels past the Confederate batteries at Vicksburg to rejoin Grant's land forces at Hard Times. All the vessels were hit repeatedly, but only one was sunk. A few nights later, six transports and 12 barges ran the same gauntlet with a large consignment of supplies. On that occasion, one transport and all 12 barges were lost.

steamers used on the bayous, the Federal forces concentrated at Hard Times. On the night of April 16, Porter tried to run 12 vessels past the batteries of Vicksburg. One vessel was sunk and the others were hit repeatedly, but the surviving 11 were able to join Grant at Hard Times, from where it was hoped to cross to Grand Gulf on the southern side of the Big Black River's junction with the Mississippi River. Porter's gunboats attacked Grand Gulf on April 29, but found the defenses too strong for any landing attempt. Grant then decided to land at Rodney, but on learning that a good road led inland from Bruinsburg, switched the landing spot to this closer town. Starting on April 30, the two corps were ferried to Bruinsburg without opposition. On the same day, Grant ordered Sherman to bring the bulk

the Seventh Ill left with Lieutenant-Colonel Blackburn (mortally wounded in one of the expedition's four actions), and 9 men missing, supposed to have straggled.''

Deceived as to the size and intent of the raiding force, Pemberton detached all his cavalry and some of his infantry in a vain attempt to intercept and destroy Grierson's force. He was also unwilling to weaken Major General Franklin Gardner's 16,000-man garrison of Port Hudson, whose vital importance to the Confederacy had been stressed by President Jefferson Davis. As he also had 7,000 men to the north under Loring to guard against any Federal advance from Tennessee on Grenada, Pemberton therefore had forces scattered all over western Mississippi and northern Louisiana. He simply could not challenge the steady development of the major threat to Vicksburg. Pemberton was also hindered by the nature of his instructions: Davis had ordered him to hold Vicksburg at all costs, while Johnston recognized that Vicksburg could be a trap for immobile forces and had therefore urged Pemberton to move out and tackle Grant. Pem-

berton tried to compromise. He began to gather his forces along the Big Black River, where they could fall back on Vicksburg if necessary, but were in position to attack the Federal lines of communication with the Mississippi River should Grant decide to attack Jackson, the state capital.

Grant Moves Toward Jackson

McClernand delayed moving inland from Bruinsburg. It was late on the morning of May 1 before his leading elements attacked the Confederate brigades protecting Port Gibson, where the road and rail bridges provided a crossing of Bayou Pierre's North Fork for an advance on Grand Gulf. The Confederates were finally threatened by a Federal outflanking movement and pulled back, destroying the bridges over the South and North Forks of Bayou Pierre as they went. This bought enough time for Bowen to evacuate the Confederate garrison of Grand Gulf before the arrival of Grant's men on May 2. By May 7, events were shaping up for the decisive phase of the Vicksburg campaign. Pemberton was

Vicksburg

For further references
see pages
7, 8, 9, 10, 11, 12, *13*, *18*,
19, 20, *21*, 25, 26, 28, 39,
40, 57, 58, 75, 117

Mississippi River

For further references
see pages
6, 7, 8, 10, 11, 12, 15, *16*,
26, 28, 39, 69, 76, 80, *97*,
117, 131

Colt Third Model Hartford Dragoon Pistol

Just under half of the total Dragoon pistol production, some 10,500 weapons, were of the Third Model. The percussion-cap weapon was made between 1851 and 1861. The weapon was also known as the Holster Pistol (the term revolver had not come into use). It was a 0.44-inch caliber weapon with a six-chamber cylinder, and weighed 4 lb. 1 oz. The type was the only Dragoon with alternative barrel lengths (7½ and the rarer 8 inch). About 1,000 were completed as pistol carbines with a detachable shoulder stock. This weapon has a particularly beautiful decorative finish.

calling back to Vicksburg all the Confederate forces scattered through Mississippi, while Grant had Sherman's XV Corps at Grand Gulf on his left wing, McPherson's XVII Corps north of Willow Springs in his center, and McClernand's XIII Corps at Rocky Springs on his right wing.

Grant had told Halleck that he would detach one corps (probably that of McClernand) to aid Banks in the capture of Port Hudson. Banks and McClernand would then rejoin the two other corps still at Grand Gulf to provide the striking force for the climax of Grant's offensive plan. However, Banks had launched a senseless expedition up the Red River on the western side of the Mississippi River. He was in no position either to attack Port Hudson or to move to Grant's aid from Baton Rouge until May 10, and then he only had 15,000 men.

A very difficult decision faced Grant. On one hand, if he waited for Banks, Pemberton might be reinforced to the extent that Vicksburg was too strong for Federal assault; on the other, an attack without Banks would leave the Federal lines of communication open to Confederate destruction. Grant made the courageous decision to abandon his lines of communication and live off the land during an immediate offensive. All available wagons (two to each regiment) were ferried across to the eastern side of the Mississippi River and loaded with ammunition, as were all vehicles and draft animals that could be seized locally, and Sherman was ordered to bring up 120 wagons loaded with salt, sugar, coffee, and hardtack.

Grant was faced with Pemberton's concentration around Vicksburg and Johnston's in Jackson. He decided to move his force between the two Confederate groups, and then destroy the one at Jackson before turning his attention to Vicksburg. The Federal forces began their offensive on May 11 from positions around Rocky Springs.

Large-scale Movements

The following day, McClernand's and Sherman's corps were located along Fourteen Mile Creek, and McPherson's corps had pushed into Raymond, thereby separating the forces of Pemberton and Johnston. During the night of May 12, Grant concluded that Pemberton was concentrating his strength at Edward's Station, about one-third of the way from Vicksburg to Jackson on the Vicksburg & Jackson Railroad. By May 14, Sherman and McPherson had entered Jackson, forcing Johnston to pull his 6,000 men north up the Great Northern Railroad, while McClernand was holding Raymond and Clinton, blocking any Confederate advance from the west.

During the night of May 14, McPherson forwarded to Grant an agent-delivered copy of a message despatched by Johnston to Pemberton, ordering the latter to move forward to Clinton so that the two Confederate forces could link up.

Joseph E. Johnston

For further references see pages
16, *19*, 20, 21, 25, 26, 28, 39, 97, 101, 102

John Clifford Pemberton

For further references see pages
7, 9, 10, 12, 13, 14, 16, 18, *19*, 20, 21, *25*, 37

Grant realized that Pemberton would already be on the move and wasted no time. He decided to strike at him immediately. Grant was ideally situated, for he was squarely between the two Confederate forces. That of Johnston was retreating to the northeast, while that of Pemberton was moving forward to the southeast in an effort to strike at Grant's nonexistent lines of communication.

In fact, Pemberton had decided not to follow Johnston's plan, but to strike toward Clinton with the object of severing the Federal lines of communication. On May 15, therefore, as Sherman's corps was destroying Jackson's industries and ripping up the railroads in and around the city before moving west toward Bolton Depot to rejoin Grant's command, Pemberton had departed from Edward's Station and was approaching Champion's Hill from the west at about the time McPherson's and McClernand's corps were approaching the same point from the east and southeast respectively. Neither army was aware of the other when the two forces bivouacked on the night of May 15/16, a mere four miles apart.

The Vicksburg campaign of 1863 split the Confederacy in two, opened the Mississippi River to Federal commerce, and freed Grant's forces, which were both large and experienced, for other tasks.

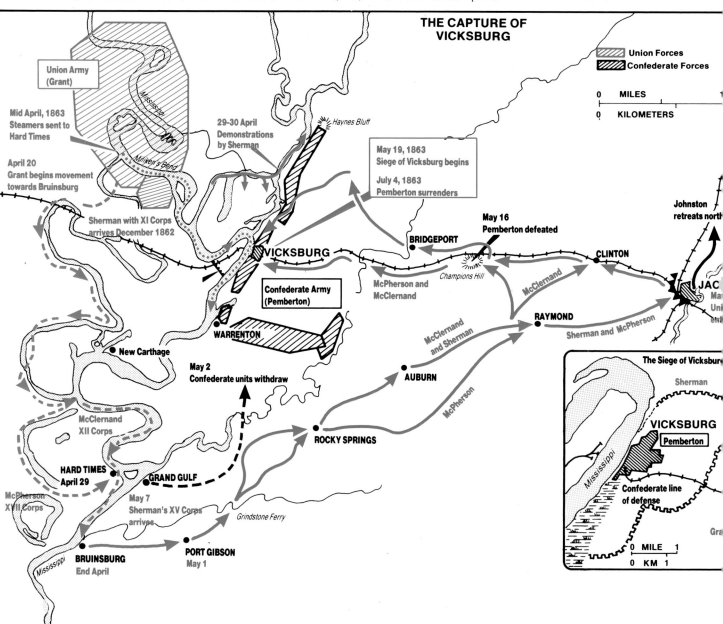

THE CAPTURE OF VICKSBURG

Union Forces
Confederate Forces

MILES
KILOMETERS

Union Army (Grant)

Mid April, 1863 Steamers sent to Hard Times

April 20 Grant begins movement towards Bruinsburg

29-30 April Demonstrations by Sherman

Haynes Bluff

May 19, 1863 Siege of Vicksburg begins

July 4, 1863 Pemberton surrenders

Johnston retreats north

May 16 Pemberton defeated

BRIDGEPORT

CLINTON

JAC

Sherman with XI Corps arrives December 1862

VICKSBURG

Champions Hill

McPherson and McClernand

McClernand

Confederate Army (Pemberton)

WARRENTON

McClernand and Sherman

RAYMOND

Sherman and McPherson

New Carthage

May 2 Confederate units withdraw

AUBURN

McPherson

The Siege of Vicksburg

Sherman

McClernand XII Corps

ROCKY SPRINGS

VICKSBURG

Pemberton

HARD TIMES April 29

GRAND GULF

Mississippi

McPherson XVII Corps

May 7 Sherman's XV Corps arrives

Grindstone Ferry

Confederate line of defense

Gra

BRUINSBURG End April

PORT GIBSON May 1

MILE
KM

First Sergeant, New York Cavalry, Union Army

This dress is typical of the non-commissioned Federal cavalry officers after the middle of the Civil War. The sky blue cavalry overcoat was a double-breasted garment with a so-called ''stand and fall'' collar. The cape was lined in yellow, the color that distinguished the cavalry, and could be thrown back over one or both shoulders to leave the arms free. When it was buttoned, the cape reached the cuff of the greatcoat. In the hands of a skilled man, the cavalry saber was an effective weapon, though the original sabre with a 42-inch blade was generally known as a ''wrist breaker.'' It was steadily replaced by a more manageable weapon with a 36-inch blade.

The Battle of Champion's Hill

The following morning, the pickets of the armies clashed, and Pemberton became aware of Grant's presence. At about the same time, Pemberton received further orders from Johnston to link up at Clinton. Pemberton realized that he could neither strike at Grant's communications nor move on Clinton, and therefore decided to pull back to Edward's Station. From there, the Confederate force could either retreat to Vicksburg or, by moving around the north of the Federal forces via Brownsville, try to join Johnston. By the time that Pemberton had made this decision, however, his force was involved in the Battle of Champion's Hill, and the decision was academic.

Involved in the battle were 21,800 Confederate and 29,000 Federal troops, the former in three divisions and the latter in seven. The Confederate position stretched south from Champion's Hill, with natural protection afforded by a ravine whose slopes up to the Confederate positions were covered with thick woods and undergrowth. Even so, the forces on the Federal right wing made good progress until Pemberton called in his two right-hand divisions to support Major General Carter Littlepage Stevenson's division on Champion's Hill. Grant ordered his extreme right-wing division to move in support of Brigadier General Alvin Peterson Hovey's division; he thereby deprived himself of the chance to cut the Confederate line of retreat. By late afternoon, Pemberton saw that his situation was impossible and ordered a withdrawal with Loring's division providing the rearguard as the divisions of Bowen and Stevenson pulled back toward Crystal Springs. The Confederates had lost 3,851 men (381 killed, about 1,800 wounded, and 1,670 missing) to the Federal side's 2,441 (410 killed, 1,844 wounded, and 187 missing).

The Vicksburg campaign was characterized by maneuver rather than combat, but nevertheless contained several small but hard-fought battles.

Right: Toward the end of the Vicksburg campaign, Grant had no alternative to formal siege. The circle of Federal lines closed around the Confederate garrison and the trapped civilians, who were then starved into surrender.

Below: The Battle of Champion's Hill on May 16, 1863, opened the way for Grant to push forward from Jackson and to lay siege of Vicksburg from the east, placing his forces between Pemberton's garrison and any relief effort by Johnston.

Pemberton Retreats to Vicksburg

At Crystal Springs, Pemberton decided that most of his men should be sent back to Vicksburg while he and 5,000 men held a bridgehead east of the Big Black River where the railroad crossed the river. As McClernand and McPherson pushed forward against Pemberton's bridgehead on May 17, Sherman headed slightly farther to the north and, crossing the Big Black River at Bridgeport on May 18, looked for a chance to cut Pemberton off while keeping watch for any intervention by Johnston.

In the bridgehead, Pemberton had evacuated much of the original force to the west bank of the Big Black River, leaving only a covering force to await the arrival of Loring's division that was retreating in front of McClernand and McPherson. The Confederate force on the

west bank of the Big Black River destroyed the bridge as the Federal forces attacked those on the eastern side, so in the Battle of the Big Black River, the Federal forces had little difficulty in capturing 1,700 prisoners and 18 guns.

The Siege of Vicksburg

Finding no sign of Johnston, Sherman pushed forward to Vicksburg, reaching the northern defenses on May 18. Grant, believing that a quick assault might gain success before the Confederates could reorganize their defenses, attacked on May 19, but was beaten back. Grant realized that a formal siege of Vicksburg would be slow, require reinforcements from Memphis, and give Johnston time to gather his strength and fall on the besieging forces' rear. He therefore ordered

The protracted siege of Vicksburg involved several features of warfare that became commonplace half a century later. One was the type of burrow city in which many of the troops lived.

John Alexander McClernand

For further references see pages 8, 9, 10, 12, 14, 15, 16, 21, 25

Overpage: The siege of Vicksburg saw comparatively little hard fighting. The surrender of the Confederate garrison eliminated the need for a Federal assault that would inevitably have been successful, but probably at very heavy cost to both sides.

The fighting for Vicksburg brought out the best in many of the soldiers involved on each side, but once the Federal army and navy had completed their investment of the city, it was only a matter of time before the Confederates had to surrender.

another attack on May 22, but it too was driven back, despite the fact that support was provided by Porter's gunboats and the army's resupplied artillery. As Grant was considering whether or not to call off the assault in the late morning, he received a message from McClernand that his troops had taken two Confederate forts. In fact, they had taken only one, and that only temporarily. Grant therefore reinforced McClernand and kept up the assault until nightfall. This senseless effort boosted the Federal casualty figure to 3,200 men.

Pemberton's army was now trapped in Vicksburg. After his defeat at the Big Black River on May 17, Pemberton had told Johnston that he was pulling back into Vicksburg. In an immediate reply, Johnston ordered Pemberton to evacuate the city if possible and thereby save his army, but on the advice of a council of war, Pemberton had decided that this was impossible. Johnston therefore ordered Pemberton to hold the city until a relief force could be gathered. This was a very difficult task for the Confederacy, given the problems faced by Bragg and General

Robert E. Lee, but a force was finally concentrated. When it started toward Vicksburg, its supposed strength was 55,000 men; real strength, however, was only 31,000 men.

Grant drew reinforcements from Hurlbut's corps and set about the wearisome task of formal siege with McClernand's, McPherson's, and Sherman's corps arranged from south to north around the perimeter. Sherman's corps also kept a vigilant watch for any move toward the relief of the Confederate garrison by Johnston. The siege involved digging approach saps, mines, and countermines as the ring was drawn tighter around Vicksburg, and there was a steady flow of casualties from sniping, artillery fire, and mines.

Grant had a maximum of 71,000 men at his disposal. Half were used in the siege itself, while the other half were kept available for operations against Johnston. On May 30, McClernand issued a congratulatory order to the men of his corps, claiming most of the successes of the Vicksburg campaign. McPherson and Sherman were furious; Sherman pointed

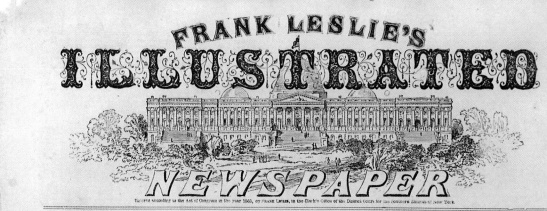

FRANK LESLIE'S ILLUSTRATED NEWSPAPER

Entered according to the Act of Congress in the year 1863, by FRANK LESLIE, in the Clerk's Office of the District Court for the Southern District of New York.

No. 410—Vol. XVI.]   NEW YORK, AUGUST 8, 1863.   [Price 8 Cents.

SURRENDER OF VICKSBURG.

Grant's Interview with Pemberton.

It has been Grant's good fortune to appear as the prominent figure in two of the three great surrenders which the rebels have been forced to make—Fort Donelson and Vicksburg.

On the 3d of July a flag of truce came into his lines brought by Major-Gen. Bowen and Col. Montgomery, with a letter from Pemberton, asking a cessation of hostilities in order to arrange terms for the surrender. Grant's characteristic reply was that his only terms were unconditional surrender. Pemberton then asked an interview, which took place at three o'clock, and the surrender was agreed upon.

The next morning Gen. Grant and his Staff met Gen. Pemberton, attended by Col. Montgomery and other officers, at the Stone House inside the rebel works, and Grant formally took possession.

The Slaves of Jefferson Davis coming on to the Camp at Vicksburg.

Few incidents have been more curious and instructive than that witnessed some time before the fall of Vicksburg, when the slaves of Jefferson Davis from his plantation on the Mississippi came into camp. It seemed in itself the doom of slavery, and formed such a contrast to the vaunt of Toombs, that he would call the roll of his slaves on Bunker Hill, that none can help being struck by it. The President of the Confederate States may call the roll of his slaves at Richmond, at Natchez, or at Niagara, but the answer will not come.

Coonskin's Observatory.

None of the sharpshooters in Grant's army has gained a more enviable reputation than Lieut. Foster, of the 2d Indiana, who erected the observatory we portray. He is the California Joe of the West. For a time, having given his cap to another officer, he wore a raccoonskin cap, and as his death-dealing rifle had made the rebels perfectly acquainted with him, they were always on the lookout for Coonskin, whose presence foreboded a speedy close of some rebel's career. His observatory overlooked the rebel works, and commanded some of their guns, so as to render it impossible to use them.

GALLANT CHARGE OF THE 6TH MICHIGAN CAVALRY

At Falling Waters, July 6.

Within the last year our cavalry has risen rapidly in efficiency, and is now, by the admission of rebel officers, far superior to theirs. The superiority of the Southern men as riders, and as cavalry, has proved as baseless as their claim to be descended from the cavaliers of England. The exploits of our cavalry in Virginia, Maryland and Pennsylvania this year would fill a volume in themselves, and rebel soldiers fly at the approach of the Northern troops more fleetly than our men ever did before the redoubtable Black Horse. Yet among the many gallant charges there are few more brilliant than that of the 6th Michigan at Falling Waters, where they rode without drawing rein right over the rebel breastworks, scattering all before them. The cavalry were not more than 50 or 60 at most, but they charged up a steep hill in the face of a terrific fire, and though they lost in killed and wounded nearly two-thirds their number, captured almost the entire force of the enemy, with three regimental battle flags.

MENDELL'S REGULAR ENGINEERS BUILDING A BRIDGE.

The Engineer service seems less brilliant than some other branches of service, and the men a kind of half soldier, half artisan. Yet when bridges are to be built, roads laid, mines run, all look to the engineer. The regular engineers work with great celerity, and in the present sketch we have an incident of Meade's pursuit of Lee, a bridge rapidly thrown over the Antietam, near Funkstown, by a body of regular engineers under Capt. Mendell, on July 11.

MORGAN'S RAID INTO INDIANA—DESTRUCTION OF DEPOT AT SALEM.

Morgan's career of plunder, rapine and destruction seems about to close. His daring invasion of Indiana drew such a force around him that his main body was forced to surrender, while he, true to his gamester antecedents, during the negotiation started off, avoiding a surrender proposed by himself,

SIEGE OF VICKSBURG—GENERAL GRANT MEETING THE REBEL GENERAL PEMBERTON AT THE STONE HOUSE INSIDE THE REBEL WORKS, ON THE MORNING OF JULY 4.—FROM A SKETCH BY OUR SPECIAL ARTIST, FRED. B. SCHELL.

Opposite: Pemberton surrenders to Grant in Vicksburg on July 4, 1863.

Below: Life in prisoner-of-war camps on both sides was generally very uncomfortable and deprived. In short, it bore very little resemblance to this idyllic scene of Federal prisoners playing baseball at Salisbury, North Carolina, during 1863. This abandoned cotton factory became a prison in November 1861. It was used for spies, Confederate soldiers awaiting court-martial, and Confederate deserters, as well as Federal prisoners of war.

out that whenever McClernand had led, it was usually in the wrong direction! On June 18, Grant replaced McClernand with Major General Edward Otho Cresap Ord and sent McClernand to an administrative command in Illinois.

Vicksburg Surrenders

Pemberton's men and the people of Vicksburg were by now close to starvation, and the Confederate strength had been reduced from 20,000 men to about 10,000 through wounds and disease. Grant ordered the preparation of a final assault, but was stalled by a Confederate request for terms on July 3. Grant had demanded unconditional surrender, but Pemberton hoped that by surrendering on the emotive day of July 4, he could gain better terms for his men. Grant allowed parole for the Confederate troops on the grounds that transporting them to prisoner of war camps would have wasted time and facilities that were better used for other purposes.

Throughout the siege of Vicksburg, Grant had worried that a Confederate relief force under Johnston might appear. So though he concentrated on capturing Vicksburg, as soon as fresh forces arrived, the Federal commander built up defenses on the northern and eastern sides of the besieging force. One division was located near the railroad bridge over the Big Black River, another was used to patrol the area as far north as Mechanicsville, Mississippi, and reconnaissance parties were sent into Confederate territory. Johnston was soon located at Canton, about 20 miles north of Jackson on the Mississippi Central Railroad line, gathering a relief force slowly.

Sherman in Command Against Johnston

By June 10, Grant had been reinforced by Major General John Grubb Parke's IX Corps, which had been sent to Cincinnati, Ohio, after the Battle of Fredericksburg. It was now brought south as the core of a

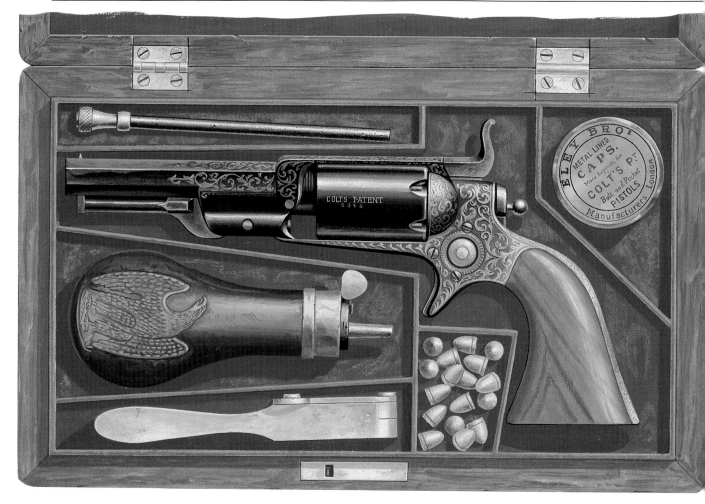

Colt Model 1855 Side Hammer Pistol

Produced in 0.265-inch and 0.31-inch calibers, this pistol had a barrel only 3.5 inches long, though the larger caliber could be supplied with a 4·5 inch barrel of round external shape. This boxed set, presented to Grand Duke Mikhail Nikolayevich of Russia, was typical, with the pistol itself surrounded (from top right) by a box of percussion caps, bullets, a bullet mold, a powder flask, and a cleaning rod.

special command, under Sherman from June 22, for the specific task of preventing any interference by Johnston in the siege of Vicksburg. Sherman was succeeded in command of XV Corps by Steele. Sherman's command occupied the region between Haynes Bluff and the railroad bridge over the Big Black River, with cavalry patrols in the quadrant from north to east to detect any Confederate movement. Additional security was provided south of the Big Black River by pickets of Ord's XIII Corps.

The only other direction from which Pemberton's garrison could have hoped for relief was the other side of the Mississippi River, where Lieutenant General Edmund Kirby Smith commanded the Confederates' Trans-Mississippi Department. Kirby Smith did try to help Pemberton with an attack on the Federal base at Miliken's Bend on June 7, but this small-scale attack was driven off without difficulty by Hurlbut's troops and Porter's gunboats.

On June 28, Johnston felt that his force was as ready as it ever would be and he advanced toward Vicksburg. On July 1, the 31,000-man Confederate force had reached the Big Black River between Birdsong's Ferry (three divisions) in the north and Edward's Station (one division) in the south. Johnston spent the next three days in reconnaissance, and on July 4 heard of Pemberton's surrender. The only sensible course left open to Johnston was a return toward Jackson.

As early as June 22, Grant had instructed Sherman to be ready to launch his pursuit at a moment's notice. Reinforced by Ord's corps, Sherman now swung onto the offensive. Johnston hurried back to the comparative safety of his prepared positions around Jackson, but Sherman refused to throw his force into a piecemeal attack that would have favored the Confederate defense. Instead, Sherman began preparation for a formal siege of the city on July 9. Johnston

2nd Lieutenant, Infantry, Union Army, 1864

In the field, many officers continued to wear the old-style frock coat with shoulder straps instead of the original epaulets. This officer also wears the regulation officer's sword belt and a pre-war type of cap box with a shield-type front flap. Regulations required each Federal regiment to have two flags, the National Flag and the Regimental Flag. This officer carries the national "Stars and Stripes," which was 6 feet 6 inches long and 6 feet along the pole. The dark blue canton contained a star for each state in the Union (33 at the beginning of the Civil War, 34 after accession of Kansas, and 35 from 1863 after West Virginia had joined the Union). The stars were silver or gold and had five, or occasionally seven, points. They were generally arranged in rows, but other arrangements were a circle, an oval, a group around one large star, and a group in the shape of one large star. The regimental title was written on the middle stripe of the 13 red and white stripes, and battle honors were sometimes added above and below. Fringe, if it was included, was yellow with mixed blue and white tassels.

decided that it would be pointless to be trapped in Jackson, and on July 16, before Sherman could complete his investment, Johnston pulled out to the east.

Port Hudson Surrenders

With the surrender of Vicksburg, further resistance by Port Hudson seemed futile. The garrison had been taken under siege by Banks on June 24 and surrendered on July 9. The siege cost Banks 3,000 casualties, but yielded 7,200 Confederate casualties (including 5,500 prisoners), two steamers, 60 guns, 5,000 small arms with 150,000 rounds of ammunition, and 45,000 pounds of gunpowder.

In overall terms, the surrender of Vicksburg came the day after the Confederate defeat at Gettysburg and sounded the death knell of the Confederacy. The Confederacy had been split in two, and all the economic and strategic advantages of control of the Mississippi River fell into the lap of the Union. It was a strategic victory of vast proportions, yet Grant had achieved it with casualties, between May 1 and July 4, of only 9,362 men. This was just one more than he (but not Buell) had suffered in the Battle of Shiloh.

A New Federal Commander in the East

Across the United States, in the eastern theater between the Atlantic Ocean and the Appalachian Mountains, the situation at the beginning of 1863 appeared good for the Confederacy, but then turned sour.

After its failure in the Battle of Fredericksburg, Virginia, Major General Ambrose Everett Burnside's Army of the Potomac went into winter quarters on the northern bank of the Rappahannock River. Lieutenant General Robert Edward Lee's Army of Northern Virginia was left in the altogether more comfortable confines of Fredericksburg, where it commanded the Federal forces' only realistic line of advance. the railroad to Richmond.

The Army of the Potomac was in very poor state. Morale was at a low ebb, threat of desertion was increasing, and the army's own administration, which had never been good, was falling apart steadily. During January 1863, Burnside's subordinate generals plotted against their commander. In many instances, they used their political connections to approach the president and Congress directly. Burnside eventually discovered what was happening and asked Lincoln to remove either him or most of his subordinates. Lincoln opted for the former course. On January 25, he replaced Burnside with Major General Joseph Hooker. The new commander of the Army of the Potomac was well regarded in Washington, but Lincoln took the unusual step of writing a letter to Hooker. In it, he warned the general about the dangers of over ambition and rashness, reprimanded him for plotting against Burnside, and asked for victories.

Hooker's first task was a thorough revision of the Army of the Potomac. A system of regular furloughs was introduced, living conditions and hospitals were improved, and measures were taken to make sure that better food reached the men regularly. This "human factor" package did much to improve morale at a time when Hooker was strengthening discipline and stepping up training, establishing an effective military intelligence apparatus, and introducing distinctive corps and division insignia to enhance the men's identification with their parent formations.

Hooker also overhauled the Army of the Potomac's structure, starting with the elimination of Burnside's grand divisions. He established seven infantry corps each with about 15,000 men, as well as one cavalry corps of three divisions under Major General George Stoneman. The cavalry had traditionally been divided into penny packets allocated to infantry corps and divisions, but Hooker regarded the cavalry as an effective fighting arm in its own right. The creation of the cavalry corps soon paid handsome dividends in increased efficiency among the Federal horse soldiers.

Throughout the winter, Major General James Edward Brown ("Jeb") Stuart's Confederate cavalry had been a thorn in

Opposite: Depicted here when he was campaigning successfully as the Democrat candidate for the governorship of Virginia in 1885, Fitzhugh Lee was a nephew of Robert E. Lee. He was born in Virginia in 1835 and graduated from the U.S. Military Academy in 1856, after narrowly avoiding dismissal by his uncle for bad behavior. He joined the Confederate army in May 1861 and served only in the eastern theater, rising to the rank of major general before he was 28. After the Civil War, he became a farmer before running for office, and after a post as U.S. Consul General to Havana between 1896 and 1898, he served in the Spanish-American War of 1898. He died in 1905.

the Federal side with a series of harassing raids on Federal outposts. Evidence of the Federal cavalry's improving capability was provided by a counter raid on March 17. Brigadier General William Woods Averell's cavalry division crossed the Rappahannock River at Kelly's Ford and drove back, though failed to destroy, Brigadier General Fitzhugh Lee's brigade of Confederate cavalry.

Not all of Hooker's alterations were good, however. A notable failure was his decision to decentralize command of the artillery to corps commanders. This meant that the Army of the Potomac was unable to call on massed artillery fire, a factor that was to play an important part in the forthcoming Battle of Chancellorsville.

Hooker's Overall Strategic Plan

Lincoln wanted victories, and Hooker was determined to provide them. Burnside's basic concept of breaking through the

Abraham Lincoln

For further references
see pages
8, 28, 37, 42, 44, *54*, 57,
58, 59, 60, 61, 63, 64, 65,
66, 67, 68, 69, 76

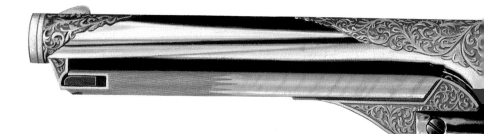

defenses at Fredericksburg to reach the Confederate capital at Richmond, Virginia, was basically sound, but these defenses had been strengthened since Burnside's failure.

Lee's defenses were based on a series of fortifications on the south bank of the Rappahannock River between Port Royal and Banks's Ford, with detached works shielding United States Ford farther upstream from Banks's Ford. Hooker knew, however, that he had considerably more men than Lee, especially as the latter had detached Lieutenant General James Longstreet with two divisions of his corps on a foraging expedition that was also designed to protect the Virginia and Carolina coasts against the landing apparently threatened by the embarkation of the Federal IX Corps onto transport ships at Hampton Roads, Virginia.

In overall terms, Hooker could call on 134,000 men. Lee had only 53,000 men, excluding Stuart's 6,500 cavalry. Hooker immediately rejected any thought of the type of frontal assault that had proved so tragically costly when Burnside attempted it at Fredericksburg. His first plan was to force Lee back from Fredericksburg by using the cavalry corps to cut Confederate communications, and then trying to trap the Army of Northern Virginia between the cavalry and the following Federal infantry. Stoneman's cavalry moved out to implement this plan, but was then stopped by dismal weather.

Classic Double Envelopment

Hooker then revised his concept into a wide-ranging double envelopment that would let strong Federal forces fall on each of Lee's flanks. In its definitive form, Hooker's plan called for three corps to cross the Rappahannock River at Kelly's Ford after moving upstream along the river's northern bank. Two other corps would demonstrate opposite Fredericksburg as a means of holding the Confederates' attention and then strike across the previous battlefield, and the other two corps would be held in reserve. The cavalry corps, minus one division that was to shield the three infantry corps moving up to Kelly's Ford, was to raid in the Confederate rear areas and thereby help to keep the Confederates off balance. The plan was first rate; unfortunately for the Federal cause, its execution was second rate.

On April 27, after demonstrations had been made at Kelly's Ford and Port Royal to keep the Confederates off balance, Major General Henry Warner Slocum led the 42,000 men of Major General George Gordon Meade's V Corps, Major General Oliver Otis Howard's XI Corps, and his own XII Corps northwest toward Kelly's Ford. The Federal force surprised the Confederate outpost at the ford on April 29, pressed southwest across the Rappahannock River, and then moved southeast across the Rapidan River at Ely's Ford (V Corps) and Germanna Ford (XIII and XII Corps).

On April 28, meanwhile, Major General John Sedgwick seized the attention of the Confederates in Fredericksburg with an ostentatious advance to the Rappahannock below Fredericksburg by Major General John Fulton Reynolds's I Corps

Colt Model 1860 Army Revolver

2,000,000 Model 1860 Army Revolvers were made between 1860 and 1873. The American government bought 129,000 of them. This percussion-cap type was of 0·44-inch caliber and had a 7·5- or 8-inch barrel, and a six-chamber cylinder. The pistol was often known as the New Model Army Pistol to differentiate it from the 1848 weapon, which then became popularly known as the Old Model Army Pistol. The Model 1860 was the most important pistol used by the Federal army in the Civil War.

and his own VI Corps. He crossed the river on April 29.

Major General Darius Nash Couch led two divisions (12,000 men) of his II Corps into concealed positions on the north side of Banks's Ford. He left Brigadier General John Gibbons's division in position just upstream of Falmouth, since its camp was visible to the Confederates, and any move would therefore be seen. The final component of the Army of the Potomac, Major General Daniel Edgar Sickles's III Corps, was alerted as army reserve, but instructed not to move from its position opposite Fredericksburg.

Lee's Decisive Response

On the other side of the front line, Lee had been planning offensive operations of his own in the Shenandoah Valley. Receiving reports of large-scale Federal moves, Lee was initially baffled by their meaning. He first thought that the corps

under Slocum's command was moving to attack Gordonsville, but the Federal advance had temporarily cut his communications with Stuart farther to the west, and his information was inadequate. Stuart had detected Slocum's move and was heading to link up with Lee, paralleling the advance of Slocum's two outer corps, but moving slightly farther to the south. On April 29, Lee shifted his three right-flank divisions closer to Fredericksburg, where they covered the bridgehead created by Sedgwick's two corps, and detached Major General Richard Heron Anderson's division to take up position near Chancellorsville, a tactically important road junction on Slocum's line of advance against Lee's left flank. Reaching Chancellorsville, Anderson decided that the position could not be held and fell back some four miles toward Tabernacle Church. Stuart meanwhile detached one brigade to keep watch on Stoneman's two cavalry divisions, whose activities had failed to perturb Lee's concentration. Moving outside Slocum's right flank, Stuart found his presence seriously impeded the speed of the Federal advance.

The Battle of Chancellorsville

By 3:00 p.m., Hooker had formidable strength near Chancellorsville in Lee's rear. Two additional divisions from Couch's II Corps were moving up to support these three corps. They had been waiting near Banks's Ford, but had then been ordered to join Slocum via United States Ford. Hooker therefore had some 54,000 men in the region of Chancellorsville, where he halted them to await further reinforcement. He would have been better advised to push forward into more open ground near

Tabernacle Church, where they could have cleared Banks's Ford for the easier arrival of reinforcements and halved their distance from Sedgwick's two corps on the other side of Fredericksburg.

On April 30, Lee received definitive information from Stuart about the strength of the Federal advance through "The Wilderness," an area of second-growth pine and oak tangled with thick underbrush, around Chancellorsville, which was itself just a single brick house. A less capable commander than Lee would have opted sensibly for a rapid withdrawal to the south when faced with such a double envelopment. Lee, on the other hand, decided on the bold strategy of meeting Hooker's double envelopment with a divided Army of Northern Virginia. Leaving Major General Jubal Anderson

The Battle of Chancellorsville on May 3, 1863, was a double-edged victory for the Confederacy: it emphasized the genius of Robert E. Lee as a tactical commander without equal, yet it cost the life of "Stonewall" Jackson, Lee's only subordinate apparently capable of understanding his plans in all their implications and fulfilling them completely.

Early with 10,000 men of Lieutenant General Thomas Jonathan ("Stonewall") Jackson's II Corps to contain Sedgwick's two corps southeast of Fredericksburg, Lee began to move the rest of his army toward Chancellorsville, where he mustered 43,000 men.

Hooker Loses the Initiative

Surprised by this Confederate reaction, Hooker pulled back and began to organize defensive positions within The Wilderness. He later admitted that this was a mistake. He had received incorrect information that Lee had been reinforced. He also thought that if Lee was determined to fight, it would be better to offer battle from prepared defensive positions so that the Confederates could bleed themselves to death. Whatever his reasons, Hooker had given the initiative to

Lee, whose strength was completed by the arrival of Jackson's II Corps from the region southeast of Fredericksburg.

The Federal position was based in the thick woods, with an abatis of felled and interlaced trees, and makeshift breastworks of timber and earth. The Federal left wing was well anchored on the Rappahannock River. But, as the Confederate right made contact with the Federal left, Stuart quickly found, and reported to Lee on May 1, the Federal right wing was hanging "in the air," it was unsupported by impassable terrain or a river and could therefore be turned. It was just the invitation that Lee needed. The Confederate commander was fully conscious of his difficult position: he was faced by considerably larger numbers and had to consider the complete inferiority of Early's position should Sedgwick go over to the offensive from his Rappahannock River bridgehead.

The Battle of Chancellorsville remains one of history's finest examples of a double envelopment. It clearly showed what can be achieved against even a well-prepared operational scheme by a supreme general using interior lines of communication to obtain maximum benefit out of smaller but highly motivated forces.

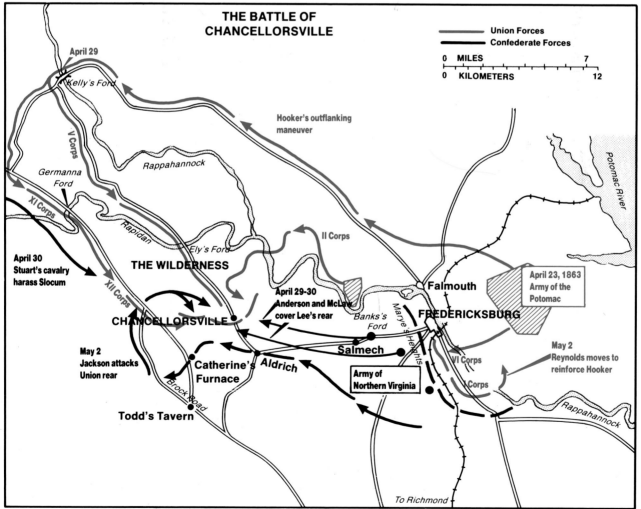

Lee's Own Plan For Envelopment

In a move of considerable boldness, Lee decided to divide his inferior force still further. While 17,000 men pinned the Federal left wing, he detached Jackson and 26,000 men to make a 15-mile march through The Wilderness and get beyond Hooker's right wing. In short, Lee's plan called for the envelopment of the original enveloper's right wing.

Jackson's force was a column ten miles long. It set off at dawn on May 2, heading first southwest and then northwest. The movement of so large a detachment could not be concealed completely, but Hooker's cavalry detachments could not penetrate the Confederates' defensive screen. The Federal commander arrived at the comfortable conclusion that the Army of Northern Virginia was beginning to retreat.

By mid-afternoon, Jackson had reached the Orange Turnpike near the Wilderness Tavern, outside and behind Hooker's left wing. Here the woods were thinner, and Jackson was able to form his men into line of battle. As he was short of

time and it was late in the day, Jackson deployed in columns of divisions, with each division deploying its brigades abreast of each other. The same type of confusing deployment had been adopted with adverse results by Johnston at the Battle of Shiloh in the previous year. Just after 5:00 p.m., Jackson's leading division fell on the outermost Federal units, and the divisions of Howard's XI Corps rolled inward toward the Federal center in complete disarray. It had been impossible for Jackson to conceal his deployment, but despite the warning of several of his officers, Howard had remained sceptical of any Confederate strength beyond this right wing until the attack fell on it. Jackson urged his men forward, but the arrival of fresh Federal forces, the poor deployment of his own men, and the onset of dusk all militated against a successful conclusion to the battle.

The Death of "Stonewall" Jackson

While searching for a track that would allow him to move part of his force to cut

The Battle of Chancellorsville, fought on difficult terrain, emphasized the importance of accurate reconnaissance. It also confirmed the uncanny intuition of commanders such as Lee and Jackson.

Hooker's line of retreat to United States Ford, Jackson was mistakenly ambushed by his own men and mortally wounded. He died eight days later, a grievous loss to the Confederate cause.

Stuart took over command of Jackson's corps, and during the night of May 2, he re-formed his line. Hooker launched attacks against Stuart's right wing, where there was a considerable gap until the left wing of Lee's forces nearer Chancellorsville. These attacks achieved considerable local success, but Hooker lacked the determination to exploit this

The dead of the 6th Maine Infantry litter the ground by the Stone Wall between Fredericksburg and Marye's Heights.

major chance to keep the Confederate detachments separated and so defeat them in detail.

Again, Hooker had yielded the initiative to the Confederates, and on the morning of May 3, he pulled his line back in the face of renewed offensive action by Stuart and Lee. During the morning, Hooker was knocked unconscious when a shell hit the pillar of the Chancellorsville house against which he was leaning. The Federal commander was thoroughly concussed for the rest of the battle, but refused to hand over command.

Just before Jackson attacked Howard's corps, Sedgwick had received Hooker's order to break out of his bridgehead and advance through Fredericksburg to Chancellorsville. Sedgwick's divisions cleared Marye's Heights at about noon on May 3, and with a superiority of about 28,000 men to 10,000, he prepared to move against Lee's rear at Chancellorsville.

Decisive and Rapid Movement by Lee

On May 4, Lee once again responded by dividing his force. Stuart was left with about 25,000 men to contain Hooker's force, which was now trapped in a bridgehead on the south bank of the Rappahannock River, with its apex at Chancellorsville and its flanks limited by the Hunting Run and Mineral Spring Run streams. Stuart maintained the Confederate pressure, and throughout the day, the Federal pocket continued to shrink back toward the river, where United States Ford was its only means of escape.

Lee moved his other 21,000 men to intercept Sedgwick. In a sharp action at Salem Church on May 3/4, Lee pushed the Federal force from its line of advance and drove it back across the Rappahannock River at Scott's Ford. With Sedgwick out of the tactical picture, Lee concentrated his force for the decisive attack on Hooker's main force during May 6. But Hooker was not prepared to fight it out, and pulled back across United States Ford, where two pontoon bridges were erected, under the rearguard protection of V Corps.

The Battle of Chancellorsville cost the

Left: In this posed photograph, a non-commissioned officer of the Federal army's engineer corps is seen with the 0·58-inch caliber Model 1861 United States Rifle Musket fitted with a fearsome 18-inch triangular bayonet. The weapon was 56 inches long with a 40-inch barrel. It weighed 9 lb. 12 oz. with the bayonet, the rate of fire was about six rounds a minute, and the effective and maximum ranges were 500 and 1,000 yards. Between January 1, 1861, and December 31, 1863, the Springfield Armory made 265,129 of these weapons.

Federals 17,300 casualties, 13 percent of the Army of the Potomac's 133,800 men, while the Confederates lost about 12,800 men, or 22 percent of the Army of Northern Virginia's 60,900 men. Yet the battle had not been a decisive victory for the Army of Northern Virginia over the Army of the Potomac, but rather a decisive victory for Lee over Hooker. It left the Army of the Potomac as a formidable fighting force, but cost the Confederacy the invaluable services of Jackson, the one man with the same type of strategic and tactical vision as Lee.

Chancellorsville: The Lessons

After the Battle of Chancellorsville, the balance of the war remained completely unchanged, and left the political and military leaders of the two sides with exactly the same problems that they had faced before the battle.

After the battle, the Army of the Potomac resumed the positions it had occupied before the battle, though Hooker was now restricted by Lincoln to the defense of Harpers Ferry and Washington. However, the president remained determined that, in the longer term, the main objective was the defeat of the Army of Northern Virginia rather than the capture of Richmond.

On the other side of the Rappahannock River, the Army of Northern Virginia was euphoric. It had won a significant tactical victory and began, unfortunately, to develop a belief in its own invincibility even against great odds. The Confederate logic was as follows: if 60,000 Confederate soldiers could defeat 134,000 Federal soldiers at Chancellorsville, then clearly the fighting capability of Confederate soldiers and the skill of their generals were so superior to those of the Federals that the numerical superiority of the northern states over the southern states was no longer significant.

The Army of Northern Virginia was in fact stronger than it had been before, for it was now reinforced to a strength of some 76,000. Conscripts arrived to swell the depleted ranks of veteran regiments, and fresh - though largely untrained - regiments arrived from the Carolinas. This

allowed Lee to reorganize the Army of Northern Virginia into three infantry corps (I, II, and III Corps commanded respectively by Longstreet, Lieutenant General Richard Stoddert Ewell,and Lieutenant General Ambrose Powell Hill) supported by Stuart's large cavalry division. Organic artillery was provided at the rate of two battalions to each corps, and one battalion to each division. The result was a flexible yet effective fighting machine whose weaknesses lay not in its front-line features, but in its lack of well-organized staffs and efficient supply services. (It is worth remembering that, for the first three years of the Civil War, Confederates units and formations up to corps level had almost double the strength of their Federal nominal counterparts.)

Lee's Reservations

One man who was not overcome by the general euphoria at the beginning of June 1863 was Lee. He realized that the position of the Confederacy was becoming increasingly more dangerous. In the eastern theater, the Army of the Potomac was still strong and would inevitably resume an offensive role against the vital political and economic areas of southern Virginia and North Carolina.

Around the periphery of the Confederacy, the Federal naval blockade of Confederate ports was becoming tighter almost by the day, and southern ports were being steadily reduced in number by a series of Federal amphibious attacks, even though the most recent (an attempt on Fort Sumter during April 7) had failed. Obviously, such raids were a drain on Federal manpower resources, but they pinned down equal numbers of the Confederacy's more limited resources. They also opened the possibility of offensives inland from these Federal beachheads,

In the northern half of the western theater, the Federal strength of 84,000 men under Rosecrans in northern Tennessee was being checked by the 45,000-man Confederate strength of Bragg, but Lee appreciated that this was a temporary stalemate. It could be easily

Private, Louisiana Tiger Zouaves, Confederate States Army

This uniform is typical of the many Zouave volunteer units raised for service on both sides. This Confederate unit, the Louisiana Tiger Zouaves was raised in New Orleans, mainly from Irish roughnecks, by Major Chatham Roberdeau "Rob" Wheat. He was the only officer who could control this unruly unit, which was known formally as Wheat's Special Battalion, or the Louisiana Zouaves. The uniform consisted of a red stocking cap with a blue tassel, a dark brown jacket with red braid in a number of patterns, a red shirt and sash, and pants made of mattress ticking (white with blue stripes or red, white, and blue stripes). The battalion had five companies, officially lettered from A to E, but unofficially called the Walker Guards, Tiger Rifles, Delta Rangers, Catahoula Guerrillas or Old Dominion Guards, and Wheat Life Guards.

Typical of Federal light artillery, this section of the Keystone Independent Battery Light Artillery (1862-63) was photographed by Matthew Brady.

overturned if more Federal forces arrived or if Rosecrans finally adopted a more offensive attitude.

Farther south in the western theater, the tide of the Mississippi campaign was definitely running against the Confederacy. Pemberton had been besieged in Vicksburg, Banks had been invested in Port Hudson, and New Orleans had already fallen to the Federal cause. This meant that only between Port Hudson and Vicksburg was it possible for the Confederacy to maintain any link with its forces west of the Mississippi River in Arkansas, Louisiana, and Texas. Added to this, a small but nonetheless grim guerrilla war was being fought in Missouri, Kansas, and Arkansas. There, the Confederate effort was being tainted by the presence among its supposed leaders of criminals such as Charles Quantrill.

Lee's inevitable conclusion was that, while he and the Army of Northern Virginia had closed the front door in the face of the Federal forces attempting to invade the Confederacy, the Federal forces were making major inroads through the back door and windows.

Another Confederate leader who saw the dangers of the Confederacy's position, perhaps with greater clarity than Lee, was Longstreet. Longstreet was farsighted enough to realize that a possible solution was for the Confederate leadership to regard the war as a strategic whole rather than as a series of separate campaigns. Longstreet's thinking was based on the fact that the Confederacy still enjoyed the advantages of interior lines of communication. The Confederacy could therefore move troops from one theater to another more quickly than the Union, which was reliant on exterior lines of communication. Longstreet's suggestion was therefore that Lee leave the corps of Ewell and Hill to contain the quiescent Army of the Potomac, move west with Longstreet's corps and all other available eastern troops to take the forces of Buckner, Bragg, and Johnston under

Robert E. Lee commanded the Confederate forces in the eastern theater from June 1862 to the end of the Civil War. From the hopelessly late date of February 1865, he was commander-in-chief of all Confederate land forces.

brigades. The 15 field artillery battalions each had four batteries.

On June 30, the Army of the Potomac had 115,250 men and 362 pieces of artillery. The army's order of battle consisted of seven infantry and one cavalry corps. The infantry corps contained 19 divisions mustering 51 brigades, while the cavalry corps had three divisions. The field artillery totaled 67 batteries assigned in brigade groupings to the corps, except for the batteries of the army reserve. The army was disposed along the Rappahannock River. Sedgwick's VI Corps maintained a small bridgehead downstream of Fredericksburg; Meade's V Corps occupied the northern bank at the junction of the Rappahannock and Rapidan rivers. The Cavalry Corps (now commanded by Major General Alfred Pleasanton in place of the unaggressive Stoneman) was upstream of V Corps along the Rappahannock, with the bulk of the army's strength (I, II, III, XI, and XII Corps) slightly farther north between VI and V Corps.

Lee Heads North Toward Pennsylvania

Early in June, Lee began his move from Fredericksburg. Leaving Hill's corps to simulate the entire Army of Northern Virginia, and so keep the Army of the Potomac in place opposite Fredericksburg, Lee planned to pass with his other two corps through the Shenandoah and Cumberland valleys, and debouch into Pennsylvania in the region of Harrisburg on the Susquehanna River. Detachments holding the passes through the Blue Ridge and South mountains provided flank protection on the eastern side of Lee's march. The task of these detachments was to protect the Confederate line of communications, as well as preventing Federal reconnaissance from discovering what was afoot.

Even though Hooker had suffered a severe failure of nerve in the Battle of Chancellorsville, he was still an acute general who was not taken in by Lee's deception. Lee's departure was soon con-

command, and then to crush Rosecrans. All this could be achieved before other Federal forces arrived to bolster him and, by paralyzing Federal activities in the western theater, could force Grant to break off his Vicksburg offensive.

It was a farsighted strategic plan, even if it did overrate the capacity of Confederate railroads, but did not appeal to Lee, who saw his primary task as the protection of Virginia.

Lee and Davis therefore decided on another Confederate invasion of the north for the same political and military reasons that had appeared valid in 1862. The Army of Northern Virginia totaled 76,225 men and 272 pieces of artillery at the end of May 1864. The army's order of battle consisted of the three infantry corps and one cavalry division, the latter now at a strength of six brigades. Each corps had three divisions, and each division generally numbered four

Flag Officer, Confederate States Navy

At the beginning of the Civil War, flag officer was the highest rank in the Confederate Navy, but was overtaken by the rank of five-star admiral in 1862. The rank is denoted by the four stars on the shoulder straps and the equivalent gold stripes on the cuff. The flag officer's undress (sea-going) frock coat was made of steel-gray cloth with facings the same color, and lined with black silk serge.

firmed by Hooker's increasingly depend-able intelligence department. By late May, Hooker knew the outlines of the Con-federate plan and soon responded with schemes of his own. On June 5, his first reaction was to wait until Lee had moved off, and then cross the Rappahannock River to destroy Hill's corps; on June 10, he revised his objective to the capture of Richmond. Both plans were overruled by Lincoln and Secretary of War Edwin Stanton, who reminded Hooker that the prime task of the Army of the Potomac was the destruction of the Army of North-ern Virginia.

To test the situation, Hooker sent Sedgwick's corps across the Rappahan-nock River on June 5/6. Sedgwick con-cluded from the strength of Hill's reac-tion that the Army of Northern Vir-ginia was still in place. Hooker's instinct told him that Sedgwick's conclusion was wrong, and he ordered Pleasanton to undertake a reconnaissance toward Cul-peper Court House on the Orange and Lexington Railroad.

The Battle of Brandy Station

As it moved toward Culpeper Court House on June 10, the Cavalry Corps ran into Stuart's cavalry division, which was at Brandy Station waiting to move north. This encounter resulted in the largest cavalry fight in American history, a very confused battle with about 10,000 men on each side. As the day wore on, the Confederates began to gain the upper hand. When Confederate infantry appeared, Pleasanton withdrew

and reported that there was substantial Confederate infantry strength, as well as cavalry in marching order, already some distance from Fredericksburg. Con-federate losses at Brandy Station were 523, and those of the Federals 936 including 486 captured. However, the Brandy Station fight was important for the Union. It was the first occasion on which the Federal cavalry had performed as well as its celebrated rival.

Hooker immediately started to move his forces west. By June 13, when it was clear that Lee was heading for the Shenandoah Valley, Hooker moved swiftly to the Manassas area. As soon as it became apparent that Hooker had left not even a rearguard at Falmouth, Hill started his corps in movement to join Lee.

Major General Robert Huston Mil-roy, commanding at Winchester in the Shenandoah Valley, reported that a Confederate raid was developing to his south. On June 10, he was ordered to fall back on Harpers Ferry. Milroy clearly did not appreciate the size of the Confederate movement and retreated too slowly. Between June 12 and 15, he was nearly overwhelmed by Ewell's corps. He lost one third of his strength and all his guns before pulling back to Maryland Heights with the remnants of his command and other Federal garrisons in the area.

By June 17, the Army of Northern Virginia was strung out over a distance of 100 miles, with the cavalry advance guard at Chambersburg, Pennsylvania, followed by Ewell's and Longstreet's corps in the Shenandoah Valley. Hill's corps was bringing up the rear as it moved into the

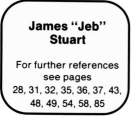

Richmond, Virginia

For further references
see pages
29, *79*, 80, *83*, 85, *88*, 97,
128

James "Jeb" Stuart

For further references
see pages
28, 31, 32, 35, 36, 37, 43,
48, 49, 54, 58, 85

Major General George Armstrong Custer's Colt Model 1860 Army Revolver.

This was a standard 0·44-inch caliber weapon complete with engraved metalwork and a grip carved with the American shield and eagle.

Shenandoah Valley via Chester Gap. By June 24, the Confederate formations had closed up considerably, with Ewell's corps around Chambersburg, Longstreet's corps around Hagerstown, and Hill's corps across the Potomac River near Shepherdstown and pushing toward Hagerstown. Stuart's cavalry, dispersed very widely, was prevented by Pleasanton's cavalry from obtaining the vital information that, on June 24, Hooker started the Army of the Potomac in motion toward Frederick, Maryland.

Stuart's Costly Diversion

On June 23, Stuart received vague orders to rejoin Lee. Stuart was smarting from southern newspaper reports that his division had been taken unawares at Brandy Station, and he planned to restore his reputation with a small, semi-independent campaign. Leaving two brigades to guard Ashby's Gap and Snicker's Gap through the Blue Ridge

Mountains, Stuart had three brigades under command. He headed north the long way around, through the Army of the Potomac's lines of communication, where he captured 150 wagons and 400 prisoners, and then went east and north around the Federal army. It was not until July 2 that Stuart finally rejoined Lee at Gettysburg, Pennsylvania, with his exhausted cavalry. The absence of his cavalry denied Lee the advantages of adequate reconnaissance during this period, and its arrival was too late to affect the outcome of the climactic battle. Hooker, on the other hand, was kept fully aware of Lee's progress and dispositions by his own scouting network.

By June 27, Hooker had concentrated the Army of the Potomac between Frederick and South Mountain, with cavalry thrown forward to Emmitsburg, Maryland, and Gettysburg. Only on June 28 did Lee belatedly learn from Longstreet, who got the information from a personal spy in Washington, that Hooker was already in position north of the Potomac River. Lee ordered his scattered Army of Northern Virginia to concentrate between Gettysburg and Cashtown, Pennsylvania.

The Replacement of Hooker

There had been considerable pressure for Lincoln to remove Hooker after the Chancellorsville debacle, but the president had decided to keep faith with his general. However, relations between Hooker and Halleck deteriorated steadily. The decisive point was Hooker's insistence that, despite his reinforcement by large parts of the Washington garrison, he was outnumbered by Lee and needed the forces at Maryland Heights. Halleck refused, on the grounds that this force represented a serious threat to Lee's line of communications, and Hooker finally asked to be replaced. On June 28, command of the Army of the Potomac was assumed by Meade, whose V Corps was taken over by Major General George Sykes. Reynolds, the commander of I Corps, had better military credentials, but Meade was selected because he was foreign-born and could therefore not use the springboard of military success to become a presidential candidate! As it

was, Meade proved an adequate choice who remained in command of the Army of the Potomac for the rest of the war.

Meade was faced with an immense task. He was opposed by Lee, the crack Confederate general who had already been the undoing of four Federal commanders, and he was poorly informed about the overall situation since Hooker had been loath to take subordinates into his confidence. Even so, on June 29, Meade pushed on to the north on a broad front, hoping to catch Lee at a disadvantage. Two days later, Major General John Buford's cavalry division, probing toward Cashtown from Gettysburg, encountered a Confederate infantry brigade heading in the opposite direction to seize a supply of shoes thought to be available in Gettysburg. Buford immediately appreciated that there were substantial Confederate forces in the area and realized that Gettysburg was the tactical key to the area as it was the junction of 12 roads.

Gettysburg: The Key Position

Leaving orders that Gettysburg was to be held at all costs, Buford reported to his corps and army commanders, Reynolds

This view of Gettysburg from the northwest shows, in the foreground, the field across which I and XI Corps retreated to reach the town and then pulled back Cemetery Hill and Culp's Hill, which are visible in the background behind the town. The road on the right is the Chambersburg Pike.

and Meade. Meade saw the value of Buford's insight. His overall scheme had been to maneuver from Frederick through Gettysburg to Harrisburg with the twin intentions of menacing Lee's line of communications and keeping his own main strength between the Army of Northern Virginia and Washington. He now decided to fight a defensive battle at Gettysburg.

The Confederate commander whose force had clashed with Buford's division outside Gettysburg was Brigadier General James Johnston Pettigrew. On receiving Pettigrew's report, Major General Henry Heth decided to move to Gettysburg with his complete formation on the following day to make sure that the desperately needed shoes were seized. The scene was set for the Battle of Gettysburg, a three-day holocaust which has aptly been described as "largely unplanned and uncontrollable...(springing) from decisions that men under pressure made in the light of imperfect knowledge." Gettysburg was to be the epitome of all the 2,000 or so land engagements of the Civil War.

Lying just to the west of Rock Creek, Gettysburg was a small town. The dominating feature was Oak Hill, northwest of the town, from which two ridges ran generally south. The longer and more easterly was Seminary Ridge, extending to the Peach Orchard and the Emmitsburg Road; the more westerly was the lower but wider McPherson's Ridge. Otherwise, the ground north of Gettysburg was level and comparatively open. South of the town, however, Cemetery Hill rose steeply to a height of 80 feet. From Cemetery Hill, a low ridge ran east to the heavily wooded Culp's Hill, while Cemetery Ridge ran one mile due south before petering out into a low wooded area with the steep hills known as Little Round Top and Round Top just to its south.

The Battle of Gettysburg

On July 1, the Battle of Gettysburg began. Federal forces north and northwest of Gettysburg resisted Confederate advances from the northwest and north. Buford's cavalrymen were acting as

mounted infantry, using their horses for mobility but dismounting for action as they sought to slow the advance of Hill's I Corps into Gettysburg. The Federal cavalry was equipped with the new Spencer breech-loading carbine and therefore possessed several times the firepower of the equivalent number of Confederate infantry. Using muzzle-loading weapons, Buford's two cavalry brigades, supported by a battery of artillery, checked Heth's advance for two hours, which bought the time necessary for Reynolds's I Corps and Howard's XI Corps to arrive in Gettysburg.

At about 11:00 a.m., Brigadier General James Wadsworth's division began to relieve the brigade of Buford's division on Seminary Ridge after arriving from Emmitsburg. The new division met Heth's attack with so furious a counterattack

Overleaf: The Battle of Gettysburg was a bloody encounter that marked the end of Confederate efforts to invade the north in the eastern theater. Fighting was confused and highlighted the difficulties of transmitting information in this period.
Below: The Battle of Gettysburg was a decisive psychological moment in the Civil War. In addition, it signaled the way in which modern warfare was evolving more than any other battle of the conflict.

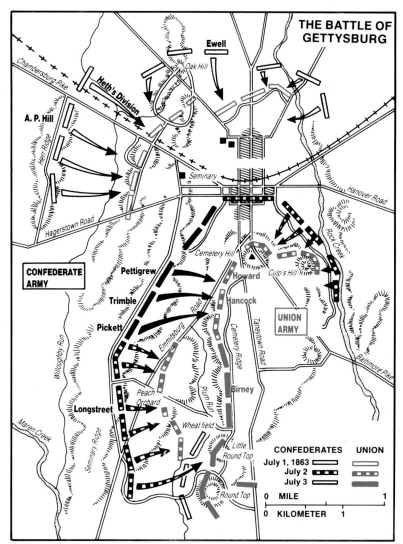

that the two leading Confederate brigades were wrecked. Reynolds was killed by a Confederate sharpshooter, and command of the Federal Corps was assumed by Major General Abner Doubleday, who organized a defensive line along McPherson's and Seminary ridges.

Growing Confederate Strength

A lull followed in this first stage of the fighting as Heth awaited the arrival of reinforcement in the form of Major General William Dorsey's division of Hill's corps. Even so, Buford's other brigade reported that it was coming under increasing pressure as Ewell's corps began to appear from the north. At about midday, Howard arrived to assume local command, passing command of his corps to Brigadier General Carl Schurz. After a rapid assessment of the situation, Howard called for support from Slocum's XII Corps and Sickles's III Corps.

Howard appreciated the tactical value of Cemetery Hill. He posted Brigadier General Adolph Wilhelm August Frederick von Steinwehr's division of XI Corps as his major reserve and began moving the corps' other two divisions toward Oak Hill on the right flank of I Corps.

At this point, Major General Robert Emmett Rodes's division, leading Ewell's corps, arrived and forced Howard to push his two right-flank divisions into line immediately north of Gettysburg. The two divisions smashed the first arrival of Rodes's division. Confederate strength was increasing rapidly, however. Hill's corps renewed its pressure from the west, Early's division arrived from York and joined the battle on Ewell's left wing to outflank the Federal right wing, and Confederate artillery was making effective use of its position on Oak Hill to enfilade both Federal corps, despite increasingly effective Federal counter battery fire. In these circumstances, the Federal line began to give. The process was slow at first, but began to look more threatening as Early's attack on the right wing gained momentum.

At about this time, Stuart's exhausted cavalry reached Dover, just west of York. The local citizens were unwilling even to

The Confederates fought with determination and dash at Gettysburg, but not even Lee's great tactical skills could prevail against the greater strength, superior weapons, and better tactical disposition of the Federal forces.

tell him that Early had recently left for Gettysburg, and Stuart reasoned that, as the Confederate invasion was apparently going well, Ewell's corps should be in the region of Harrisburg. Pausing only long enough to water his mounts, Stuart pressed on toward Carlisle.

The Federal Forces Pull Back From Gettysburg

Ewell's corps was meanwhile driving south through Gettysburg, and the now thoroughly disorganized XI Corps lost a substantial number of prisoners as it fell back. The corps' surviving infantry finally rallied behind the artillery on Cemetery Hill and Culp's Hill. The formations of I Corps also fell back, though in better order than those of XI Corps, with the left wing covered by Buford's cavalry. The two Federal corps had suffered about 50 percent casualties, but had saved almost all their artillery. Soon after 4:00 p.m., Hancock arrived in advance of his own II Corps with orders from Meade to assume overall command in Gettysburg. This order offended Howard, who was senior to Hancock, but he cooperated - if only under silent protest. Hancock saw the overall importance of Culp's Hill as the point on which the Federal right wing could be latched, and he ordered Doubleday to provide a garrison in the form of the remnants of the "Iron Brigade" from Wadsworth's division. Things began to look better for the Federal cause when XII Corps began arriving at 5:00 p.m. and III Corps at 6:00 p.m.

Ewell had pushed his corps right through Gettysburg, but Hill was content to halt once his corps had arrived on Seminary Ridge. Lee arrived at 2:00 p.m. Despite the tactical success of his two corps during the morning and early afternoon, Lee was not happy with the situation, for he had been caught in a trap of his own devising. He had invaded Pennsylvania in the hope of winning a decisive battle on northern soil, yet in the process had scattered his infantry across much of southern and central Pennsylvania, and also lost touch with his cavalry. Now his army was only half concentrated, and aggressive subordinates had forced him into a major battle not of his own planning.

Lee did not know the location of the Army of the Potomac's other corps, but had to assume that they were moving on Gettysburg as quickly as possible. He saw immediate salvation as lying in the swift destruction of I and XI Corps, and now ordered Ewell to take Cemetery Hill "if possible." Ewell considered the strength of the Federal position with its emplaced artillery, the condition of his own men after a hard approach march and battle, and a report (later shown to be false) that a Federal column was advancing onto his rear down the York road, and informed Lee that the task was not possible. Ewell's last formation, Major General Edward Johnson's division, arrived at about 7:30 p.m., but as night fell, Ewell remained steadfast in his conviction that it was too late to undertake any effort against Cemetery Hill.

The Confederate forces settled into a large arc from a point northeast of Culp's Hill, west through Gettysburg, and then south along Seminary Hill.

Meade arrived at about midnight, and during the night, the Federals used their interior line of communications to move forces onto Culp's Hill, Cemetery Hill, Cemetery Ridge, and Little Round Top.

Federal Weaknesses

On the second day of the Battle of Gettysburg, the Federal forces were faced with Confederate attacks on their southwestern and northeastern flanks. By the morning of July 2, Meade had completed the deployment of the Army of the Potomac. The Federal position was strong except in three places. First, the two Round Tops were unoccupied except by the men of a signal station on Little Round Top. Second, Pleasanton had ordered Buford back from his left wing picket position to Winchester, but he had forgotten to send forward a replacement unit. Third, Sickles, commander of III Corps, acting on his own responsibility, had shifted his position forward from the southern end of Cemetery Ridge to slightly higher ground near the Peach Orchard. This move put his corps on an exposed salient.

By early afternoon on July 2, six of the Army of the Potomac's seven infantry corps were deployed in the shape of an upside-down fish hook with a ring at the end between Round Top and Little Round Top. The shank ran north up Cemetery Ridge with Sickles's corps to its west, and the hook ran east toward Culp's Hill, with the point just south of it.

Lee had not been able to respond as rapidly; he lacked the capacity for speedy reconnaissance. Thus the first of Longstreet's divisions did not arrive until the afternoon. It took up its position on the southern end of the Confederate line, opposite the salient held by Hancock's II Corps and Sickles's III Corps.

Sherman later described 1863 as the year in which the Civil War entered its professional phase. By then, the troops were moderately well trained and usually had adequate combat experience, while officers had mastered the intricacies of their tasks and were capable of deploying their forces with the skill relevant to the day's tactical concepts.

These tactical concepts often called for the simultaneous delivery of a frontal assault and flanking or even enveloping movements. However, the numbers of men involved by 1863, together with lack of accurate timekeeping and signaling capabilities, made it difficult to execute complex maneuvers. The second day of the Battle of Gettysburg illustrates this point to a marked degree.

Lee's plan for the day involved all three of his corps: from south to north,

Bodies of the dead on the battlefield of Gettysburg.

A dead Confederate sniper, complete with his Model 1861 rifle, after the Battle of Gettysburg. This was one of several Civil War battles fought with fixed trench lines; in these circumstances, the skill of the sniper was important in keeping the enemy off balance and, if possible, to pick off his officers.

Longstreet's corps was to outflank the left wing of the Federal army and drive north into its rear area. At that point, Hill's corps, with Anderson's division in the van, was to attack the Federal center, and Ewell's corps was to wait until it heard the guns of Longstreet's corps before sweeping forward to envelop the Federal right flank.

Lee wanted an early attack, but his orders were not issued until 11:00 a.m. Longstreet was unhappy with Lee's orders, for he had suggested that the Army of Northern Virginia use the defensive possibilities of its position to tempt the Army of the Potomac into an ill-judged attack.

Poor Deployment

Meade rode to the left wing when he heard the sound of Longstreet's preliminary artillery bombardment, and only then discovered the location of Sickles' corps with its apex in the Peach Or-

chard. By then, it was too late to order the corps back to its intended position. Meade had already ordered Major General George Sykes's V Corps from its reserve position to support Sickles and now started to move large elements of XII Corps to the left wing. The leading elements of VI Corps were arriving, but after a 34-mile march, they were too tired for immediate use.

The fighting did not begin until 4:00 p.m., for Longstreet had considerable difficulty in deploying his corps on unfamiliar ground against an enemy position that was not where he had expected. Longstreet's deployment was undertaken on formal lines, with the brigade as its basic maneuver unit and each brigade disposed with its regiments in a two-rank line. The divisions advanced in columns of brigades, with intervals of between 150 and 300 yards separating the brigades, and skirmishers protecting the flanks of any units which had no immediate neighbor.

As in most wars, this deployment

lasted no longer than the beginning of the approach to Little Round Top. The actual attack was undertaken by divisions and brigades which arrived piecemeal, but then committed themselves with huge determination.

The attack started with the regiments in close order since the men were generally equipped with muzzleloading weapons and had to stand shoulder to shoulder to secure effective firepower and shock effect. Once the regiments were under Federal fire, the intervals between units began to lengthen, and the men of individual units often scattered for cover behind stone walls and trees. Soon the tactics of this grim battlefield had degenerated into short rushes under the covering fire of neighboring units. By late afternoon, the battlefield around the Round Tops was a smoke-shrouded confusion of tangled battle lines and agonized casualties awaiting rescue.

On the extreme right of the Confederate line, Major General John Bell Hood's division shattered the left flank of III Corps, overran the Devil's Den below the Little Round Top, and started a desperate advance up the western slope of the Little Round Top. In Confederate hands, this would have been a decisive feature, for though it was lower than the heavily wooded Round Top, the recent clearing of its western and northern slopes provided excellent fields of fire from which the Confederate artillery could have bombarded the Federal line.

The Fight for Little Round Top

At this point, Meade's chief engineer, Brigadier General Gouverneur Kemble Warren, discovered that Little Round Top lacked any infantry protection. On his own responsibility, Warren ordered V Corps to send up two infantry brigades and a battery of artillery. This Federal force arrived just seconds before the leading wave of Hood's division, and desperate fighting prevented the Confederates from taking the summit of Little Round Top.

The center and right of III Corps held slightly longer, but were then compelled to fall back. At this point, Anderson's division joined the Confederate offensive; but its attack was poorly executed and, after breaking through the Federal center, it was driven back.

On the other side of the battlefield, Ewell's guns opened fire when they heard Longstreet's artillery, but were soon silenced by Federal counter battery fire. It was nearly nightfall before Ewell committed his infantry. Johnson's division occupied some empty trenches at the bottom of Culp's Hill, but could not take the hill itself. Early's division attacked up the eastern side of Cemetery Hill, and although two brigades reached the top, they were driven back with enormous losses.

The third day of the Battle of Gettysburg was marked by a final, indeed despairing, effort against the Federal center from the west. As the fighting died away for the night on July 2, Meade called a council of war to help him consider whether to retreat or to stay and fight. All the corps commanders opted for the latter course, and Meade decided to remain in position and fight a defensive battle. Considering the options open to Lee, Meade decided that as the commander of the Army of Northern Virginia had already launched attacks on the Federal right and left, he would now try a decisive blow against the Federal center.

Despite the advice of Longstreet, who urged an envelopment of the Federal left wing so that the Army of Northern Virginia could get across the Federal lines of communication and force the Army of the Potomac to attack, Lee decided to maintain his own offensive. The factors that swayed him to this ultimately fatal decision were the vulnerability of his own communications and lack of time. The Confederates were living off the land, and they had exhausted all the food and fodder in the Gettysburg area. Lee originally planned a general assault all along the Federal line, but then changed his mind and ordered a concentrated effort against II Corps in the Federal center while Stuart's cavalry, which had finally arrived, struck at the Army of the Potomac's communications.

Slocum also took advantage of the dark to regroup his XII Corps around Culp's Hill, and on the other side of the

Corporal, Artillery (Richmond Howitzers),
Confederate States Army, 1865

Artillery for the Confederate States Army was always in short supply, and militia companies such as the Richmond Howitzers had to make do with their own pre-war weapons, most of them obsolete pieces dating from before the War of 1812. This corporal carries a double-ended tool with a rammer at one end and a worm at the other. In addition to captured Federal pants (reinforced for use on horseback), he wears a kepi, a shell-jacket, and a haversack. The kepi was an economy item without a chinstrap. Its peak was made of layers of thin cardboard glued together, covered in black cloth, and edged with leather binding. The jacket of homespun, and probably homemade, but properly finished with brass buttons and tape trim in the artillery's distinguishing color red. The leather haversack was intended for carrying powder cartridges from the limber or ammunition wagon to the gun, but was often used for other purposes.

Colt Model 1851 Navy Pistol

Seen here as a highly decorated weapon with a cameo of Abraham Lincoln on the handle, the Model 1851 Navy Pistol was also known as the Belt Pistol. Some 215,348 Model 1851s were produced up to 1865. The weapon was of 0·36-inch caliber, weighed 2 lb. 10 oz., and had a six-chamber cylinder. The standard barrel was 7½ inches long, though weapons with barrels as short as 5¼ inches and as long as 12 inches were also made to special order. Some examples could also be fitted with a shoulder stock. The Model 1851 was very popular in the Confederacy and was the pattern on which most southern copies of Colt pistols were based.

front line, Johnson's division was reinforced with three more brigades for a final effort to take this position. Johnson attacked, but, by 11:00 a.m. on July 3, he had been driven back to his original positions.

Preceded by a massive artillery bombardment, the final Confederate assault was to be delivered by the 47 regiments of 10 brigades of four divisions from Longstreet's and Hill's corps. The core of this force was provided by Lee's last uncommitted formation, Major General George Edward Pickett's division.

At 1:00 p.m., 159 Confederate guns opened fire and were answered by a smaller number of Federal guns. At about 2:00 p.m., the Federal guns ceased fire to conserve their ammunition, and the Confederate gunners, almost out of ammunition and believing they had silenced the opposing guns, urged the infantry to advance.

"Pickett's Charge"

Some 15,000 Confederate infantry emerged from the woods on Seminary Ridge, dressed their three lines into parade-ground formality, and began their 20-minute movement to Cemetery Ridge. The Confederates marched almost all of the way, breaking into a run only in the last stages. That the Federal guns had not been silenced became clear as they started to decimate the Confederate force. Particular damage was done by the 40 Napoleons on the southern end of the ridge, and by the smaller number of rifled guns on Little Round Top. The enfilading fire tore huge swathes through the gray-clad lines, but the Confederate

infantry closed the gaps and came on regardless, even though the weight of the fire from the south pushed Pickett's right wing in toward the center.

Despite their losses, the Confederates kept in formation until they reached rifle and canister range of II Corps. Then, the devastation of this close-range fire finally caused the Confederates to lose cohesion. The four brigades on the left of Pickett's first line were particularly hard hit, but nonetheless managed to reach and cross the stone wall defended by Major General John Gibbons' division before being killed or captured. As the Federal forces closed on Pickett's force, some of the Confederates surrendered, some ran, and many died before the survivors regained the sanctuary of the woods on Seminary Ridge.

Stuart was unable to play any effective part in the battle, for his exhausted horsemen were intercepted and halted well to the east of the battlefield by three Federal brigades commanded by Colonel John Irvin Gregg.

That "Pickett's Charge" was the turning point in the Civil War, or even the effective end of the Battle of Gettysburg, seems not to have penetrated the minds of the Confederate commanders. Longstreet rallied the survivors and marshaled them into the defensive deployment in anticipation of a Federal counterattack.

Despite the fact that he had been seriously wounded in "Pickett's Charge," Hancock urged just such a move by V Corps and the fresh VI Corps. Meade had committed himself to a defensive battle, however, and had no plans to take the offensive, especially as the formations of

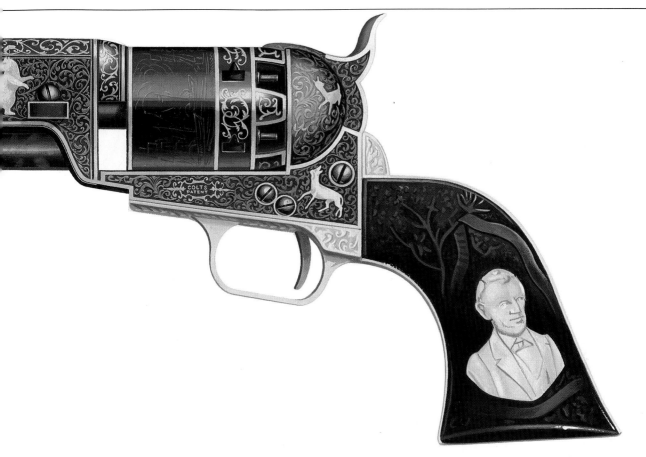

Lee Hurt But Not Crushed

During the evening of July 3, Lee pulled his crushed army together and dug in along the line from Oak Hill to the Peach Orchard. It had been a devastating three days for the two armies. Of some 88,290 Federal soldiers involved, 23,049 had become casualties (3,155 killed, 14,529 wounded, and 5,365 missing), while the equivalent casualty toll for the 75,000 Confederate soldiers had been 28,063 (3,903 killed, 18,735 wounded, and 5,425 missing).

Gettysburg was a victory of huge strategic and psychological importance for the Federal cause. It was also Lee's worst defeat. Yet, despite manifest errors such as the sacrifice of some of his best infantry in an effort to win a battle that was already lost, Lee did not lose his nerve or decline from his otherwise extraordinarily high standards of generalship.

Lee saw that his invasion of the north had again ended in failure and that he had to pull back. Nevertheless, on July 4, Lee held his positions and defied Meade to attack. Meade declined, which was a great boost to the morale of the Army of Northern Virginia. As the armies faced each other, Lee started his casualties off on the long road south. In driving rain during the night of July 4/5, Lee pulled his army back toward Hagerstown.

Meade had spent July 4 reorganizing his forces and planned to undertake a reconnaissance in force on the following day. By this time, Lee had disappeared.

Chance to Cut Off the Army of Northern Virginia

Throughout the Gettysburg battle, a small Federal force under Major General William Henry French had been located at Frederick. On July 3, French dispatched a force to raid the Confederate pontoon bridge over the Potomac River at Falling Waters. Surprising the bridge's small guard, the Federal force destroyed the bridge, and as the river was rising steadily

A wounded Zouave receives water in a deserted camp in this Matthew Brady photograph. Deaths off the battlefield exceeded those on the battlefield by a considerable margin in the Civil War; one of the many reasons was contaminated water.

after heavy rain, opened the possibility that the Army of Northern Virginia might be trapped on the northern side of the river.

Having sent his army's train toward Hagerstown the long way via Chambersburg under escort of a cavalry brigade to prevent the Federal cavalry from intercepting it, Lee was retreating over the shorter southern route directly to Hagerstown. Meade did not pursue directly, but was content to send one cavalry brigade (later reinforced by an infantry brigade detached at Emmitsburg) to shadow Lee as the Army of the Potomac headed for Frederick, and only then turned toward Hagerstown. The Federal progress was ponderous and was slowed still further by the heavy rain. Meade became concerned that Con-

federate strength was greater than he thought and that Lee might turn and fight again, so he failed to press his potential advantage.

Lee arrived in Williamsport on July 7. The Army of Northern Virginia was almost out of ammunition, and the loss of stragglers and deserters had reduced his strength to about 35,000. Lee's position was critical. As part of his force prepared an entrenched position with its back to the river, the rest tore down Williamsport's warehouses to improvise a bridge.

On July 12, Meade's 85,000 men approached the Confederate position and halted. Meade called a council of war to help him decide on the Army of the Potomac's course of action. His more aggressive corps commanders (Hancock, Reynolds, and Sickles) were

ern theater during 1863. Meade and Lee continued to maneuver against each other in Virginia for the rest of the year in the Wilderness campaign, but the focus of strategic importance now moved west into Tennessee.

In this theater, the last major event had been the Battle of Stones River during January 1863. After his reverse in this battle, Bragg pulled the Army of Tennessee back southeast of Murfreesboro in southern Tennessee and deployed his two corps in strong defensive positions covering the line of any Federal advance to the Tennessee River in the region of Chattanooga. Lieutenant General Leonidas Polk's corps was on the left around Shelbyville, and Lieutenant General William Joseph Hardee's corps on the right around Wartrace. Warning of any Federal advance would be provided by infantry outposts across his front and cavalry outposts stretching well into the areas through which any outflanking or enveloping movements would have to pass.

On the other side of the front line, Major General William Starke Rosecrans seemed content to remain in the area around Murfreesboro with his Army of the Cumberland.

Bragg on the Strategic Defensive

Bragg was both outnumbered and unlikely to receive any useful reinforcement as long as Vicksburg held Confederate attention in the western theater. He therefore had to remain on the defensive. His major objective was to prevent any Federal movement against Chattanooga, which was vital to the Confederacy as the major road and rail junction in the region. Bragg was also keenly aware that the Federal capture of Chattanooga would not only throttle one of the Confederacy's main east-west lines of communication, but also open a way through the barrier of the Allegheny Mountains to the south and provide a springboard for an advance southeast into Georgia or northeast into eastern Tennessee, whose pro-Union inhabitants Lincoln had long wished to rescue from the Confederacy.

The reverse of this situation was valid for Rosecrans, of course. Throughout the

either dead or wounded, and the current commanders urged Meade not to attack.

Lee Escapes to Fight Another Day

Thus Lee was able to evacuate the remnants of the Army of Northern Virginia across the Potomac River on July 13/14 in a move that took Meade completely by surprise. At the last minute, Buford and Brigadier General Hugh Judson Kilpatrick, Meade's ablest cavalry commanders, sensed what was happening and fell on Heth's rearguard at Falling Waters, driving the last Confederates into the river and capturing 500 prisoners as well as two guns.

The Battle of Gettysburg was the last major battle of the war in the east-

Nathan Bedford Forrest

For further references
see pages
7, 8, 67, 118, 120, 121

late winter and spring of 1863, Halleck and Lincoln constantly urged Rosecrans to go over to the offensive. Rosecrans steadily refused to be prodded into action, offering a number of lame excuses. One of the more far-fetched (but most frequently offered) was the suggestion that a Federal offensive might force Bragg to pull back and join forces with Pemberton, thereby complicating Grant's task at Vicksburg. Halleck finally threatened to replace Rosecrans if his army did not move out against Bragg, but Rosecrans refused to be threatened into action, and Halleck finally restricted his action to complaining about ''the expense to which (Rosecrans) put the government for telegrams.''

The period was not completely without activity, however, for both Rosecrans and Bragg devoted much attention to cavalry raids deep in the enemy's territory. In February 1863, Major General Joseph Wheeler's division of Confederate cavalry raided toward Fort Donelson, but failed. In March, Rosecrans dispatched Federal cavalry to cut Bragg's lines of communication, but lost the force. Major General Nathan Bedford Forrest headed a Confederate effort to cut Rosecrans's lines of communication, but failed. Colonel John Tyler Morgan led a force of 2,460 Confederate cavalry deep into Ohio and Pennsylvania on a classic raid that ended with the capture of Morgan and his last 365 men on July 26. The Confederate effort did cause Rosecrans some worry about his lines of communication, but cost 4,000 men. The Federal effort worried Bragg little, and cost 3,300 men.

Rosecrans Takes the Offensive

Rosecrans was finally ready for action on June 26. His men were well trained and well equipped, and Rosecrans had devised a sound basic strategy. Major General David Sloan Stanley's cavalry corps and Brigadier General Robert Seamen Granger's Reserve Corps were to move forward on the Federal right wing into open country with the purpose of persuading Bragg that this was the main Federal effort, directed against Shelbyville. Meanwhile, the main

effort would actually be made in the left wing, where General Alexander McDowell McCook's XX Corps, General George Henry Thomas's XVI Corps, and General Thomas Leonidas Crittenden's XXI Corps were to pass through the passes and difficult terrain to the east with the intention of turning Bragg's unsuspecting right flank.

The advance by 56,000 infantry and 9,000 cavalry was extremely difficult. Heavy rain turned every road and track into a deep quagmire, but Rosecrans's strategy worked admirably. The Federal forces pushed past the Confederate outposts after some stiff fights in the mountain gaps, and by June 30, the Army of the Cumberland had reached Manchester, while Bragg had pulled his two infantry corps, Stuart's cavalry, and what survived of the outpost line, back into Tullahoma on the main railroad line south from Murfreesboro.

The ''Tullahoma Maneuver''

Rosecrans may have been slow to move in the first place, but once he was under way, he was capable of very swift movement. Rosecrans tried to seize the crossing of the Elk River in Bragg's rear and so trap the Army of Tennessee, but by abandoning part of his stores and artillery, the Confederate commander fell back just in time. However, so rapid and close was the Federal pursuit that Bragg felt it impossible to halt in the next defensive position, the mountains between the Elk and Tennessee rivers. He therefore fell back all the way to Chattanooga, where the Army of Tennessee arrived on July 4.

Known as the ''Tullahoma Maneuver,'' this initial stage of the Federal offensive had been remarkably successful. In a mere nine days, Rosecrans had forced the Army of Tennessee back across the Tennessee, and in the process suffered only 560 casualties.

The Confederate government considered an offensive to retake that part of Tennessee that had been lost so simply, but then rejected the concept as impractical. Instead, it decided that Chattanooga must be held at all costs. In the shorter term, the Army of Tennessee's strength of

30,000 infantry and 14,000 cavalry was bolstered by subordinating Major General Simon Bolivar Buckner's 9,000-man corps, which had been located in strategic pockets along the upper reaches of the Tennessee River, but was now closing up toward Chattanooga. In the longer term, the Army of Tennessee was to be further reinforced, if necessary, from the Army of Northern Virginia in the form of Longstreet's corps after its return to Virginia after the disaster at Gettysburg.

Chattanooga: Vital to the Confederacy

Before these forces could reach him, Bragg prepared the defense of Chat-

tanooga with the assets at hand. The city itself was entrusted to Polk's corps, and the railroad line between Chattanooga and Cleveland farther to the east became the responsibility of Hardee's corps. One infantry brigade held a bridgehead over the Tennessee River at Bridgeport, where the main rail line to the west crossed the river; and the cavalry was thrown out as flank guards, with Wheeler's and Forrest's corps located west and east of Chattanooga respectively. The cavalry was on the south side of the river, however, and could not therefore undertake any reconnaissance of Rosecrans's dispositions and movements.

On the north side of the river, Rosecrans had halted during July 4 with his forces on the line between Fayetteville

Part of Federal strategy in the war was the capture of the Confederacy's ports. A major objective was Charleston. In an effort to isolate the city from the sea, Federal forces attacked Morris Island on July 10, 1863. The island's main defense was Fort Wagner. On July 18, the 54th Massachusetts Colored Infantry opened the way into the fort. The Federal forces were unable to maintain the advantage and were driven back.

59

and McMinnville via Decherd. The Army of the Cumberland remained on this line until August 15; the only move was the detachment of Major General Philip Henry Sheridan's division from XX Corps to take Stevenson, which Rosecrans needed as his railhead. Again, Lincoln and Halleck were furious about Rosecrans's lack of activity and urged an immediate attack on Chattanooga. Rosecrans replied that he had to wait until the corn was ripe, the railroad to Stevenson repaired, and flank support provided on his right by Grant and on his left by Major General Ambrose Everett Burnside's Army of the Ohio, which should advance from Cincinnati to Knoxville.

Halleck thought that so much strength was unnecessary, and that the delay would give the Confederates the chance to reinforce Bragg. On August 4, Halleck ordered Rosecrans to advance, but it was only on August 16 that the Army of the Cumberland moved. The fact that Rosecrans had kept his army well back from the Tennessee River meant that Bragg could not even guess the most likely spot for the Federal crossing.

Rosecrans had two options: upstream of Chattanooga, where it would be easier for Polk's and Hardee's corps to reach him, or downstream of the city, where it would be more difficult for the two Confederate corps to reach the crossing point, and where he would be closer to his vital rail communications. While three brigades of XXI Corps demonstrated upstream of Chattanooga to sow confusion in Bragg's mind, the rest of the Army of the Cumberland concentrated near Stevenson by August 20 and immediately started to cross the river at Caperton's Ferry. A week later Bragg belatedly realized that this was the main crossing, for he had been sure that Rosecrans would cooperate with Burnside east of Chattanooga, a belief that the Federal demonstrations upstream of the city seemed to confirm.

Rosecrans Crosses the Tennessee River

Rosecrans had secured complete tactical surprise. He got his whole army across

The Battle of Lookout Mountain, fought on November 24, 1863, in the Chattanooga campaign, became known as the Battle Above the Clouds after the Civil War. A thick blanket of fog rolled over the battlefield after the first phase of the fighting.

Ambrose Everett Burnside

For further references see pages
28, 29, 30, 68, 70, 71, 80

the Tennessee River by September 4, using first Caperton's Ferry and then Bridgeport and Shellmound. Now he faced the problem of crossing a difficult series of ridges, valleys, and streams before the Army of the Cumberland (minus the Reserve Corps left to protect the crossing and Rosecrans's line of communications) reached the more open country through which the Western and Atlantic Railroad ran. From here, Rosecrans planned to turn toward Chattanooga and trap the Army of Tennessee against the river.

Once he overcame his initial surprise, Bragg swung into action, and Buckner's corps was soon moving toward Chattanooga. On September 4, Major General William Henry Talbot Walker's division left Johnston's command to move to Chattanooga, and on the following day, Longstreet's corps received orders to move from Virginia. Longstreet's corps mustered some 15,000 men and six batteries of artillery, but as Burnside had seized Knoxville, the corps had to be routed via Savannah, Augusta, and Atlanta in a 900-mile railroad trip that

delivered the corps to Chattanooga on September 18.

Bragg saw what Rosecrans was trying to achieve. He slipped out of Chattanooga to the south, planting rumors that the Army of Tennessee was completely demoralized and running for its life. Rosecrans decided to pursue. This decision would perhaps have been wise, given the very difficult nature of the terrain, if the Confederates really had been in disorganized flight toward Dalton on the Western and Atlantic Railroad. Rosecrans drifted from his normal caution and allowed his corps to move in a pattern that would separate them beyond any chance of mutual support.

There were only a few passes through the mountains, and no useful lateral roads. So Rosecrans spread his army in three columns over a 40-mile front, with McCook's XX Corps moving via Valley Head toward Winston's Gap in Lookout Mountain before concentrating at Alpine. Thomas's XIV Corps advanced via Trenton toward Stevens's Gap before concentrating southwest of Pond Spring to prepare for an advance on Resaca

Wheeler undertook a raid into the Federal rear area between October 1 and 9, 1863, during Rosecrans's Chattanooga campaign. It was designed to sever the Federal forces' extended lines of communication. This typical episode of the raid shows the Confederate cavalry attacking a Federal wagon train near Jasper, Tennessee.

Drummer, 88th New York Volunteer Infantry Regiment, Irish Brigade, Union Army, 1864

When it was first organized, the Irish Brigade (1st Division, II Corps, Army of the Potomac) was made up of three New York volunteer regiments, the 63rd, 69th, and 88th. However, in the fall of 1862, the 28th Massachusetts and 116th Pennsylvania Regiments were added, and the 29th Massachusetts Regiment served with the brigade during the Peninsular and Antietam campaigns. In September 1864 the remnants of the 7th New York Heavy Artillery were added to the brigade, whose regiments each carried a green regimental flag. The brigade's regiments also wore a distinctive uniform. It included gray pants, the regulation fatigue coat modified with a green collar and green cuffs, and a red cloverleaf badge on top of the kepi.

As in all wars, the periods of tedious camp life far exceeded those of active campaigning and fighting. It was important for the morale of the men to be maintained at a high level, and this need led to occasions such as this "stag dance."

intended to cut the Army of Tennessee's line of retreat to the south. Crittenden's XXI Corps headed via the railroad route to concentrate at Chattanooga before turning in pursuit of the Army of Tennessee down the railroad via Ringgold.

Rosecrans's Preoccupation With Flank Defense

Rosecrans was particularly worried by his right flank, which was exposed to the south. He therefore allocated to McCook all his cavalry, with the exception of one brigade, which he gave to Crittenden to supplement a single infantry brigade, which he had previously converted to mounted infantry in an effort to reduce his cavalry shortage. The effect of Rosecrans's preoccupation with his flanks was that Thomas, in the center, lacked any cavalry screening.

Bragg's withdrawal from Chattanooga was complete by September 8, and the Army of Tennessee now concentrated around Lafayette, Georgia. At this point, Hardee was replaced by Lieutenant General Daniel Harvey Hill, fresh from Virginia. Hill deployed one of his divisions to slow Thomas's advance, and Bragg undertook a similar task against

McCook and Crittenden with Wheeler's and Forrest's cavalry corps. Bragg was able to build up a good picture of Rosecrans's strength and dispositions. On September 9, he ordered an attack on the rear of Major General James Scott Negley's division, which was leading XIV Corps, by Major General Thomas Carmichael Hindman's division of Polk's corps, while the Federal division was engaged frontally by Hill's corps. Hill was slow and found a string of excuses not to attack, so Bragg ordered Buckner's corps to join Hindman's division for a major assault on Negley's rear.

Hindman was worried about the whereabouts of McCook and Crittenden and moved only at a snail's pace even when he was ordered to attack on September 10. Bragg compounded Hindman's fears by informing him of the two other Federal corps' positions. Hindman thus began to feel that he was advancing into a trap, especially when he was informed by Bragg that the Federals had a strength of 15,000 at Dug Gap, where his 8,000 men were to attack Negley's division. Hindman therefore pulled back, and only when he learned that Bragg's information was wrong did he march forward again. The waste of time allowed the now thoroughly alarmed

U.S. Army Civil War Campaign Streamers

Sumter	April 12-13, 1861
Bull Run	July 16-22, 1861
Henry and Donelson	February 6-16, 1862
Mississippi River	February 6, 1862 - July 17, 1862
Peninsular	March 17 - August 3, 1862
Shiloh	April 6-7, 1862
Valley	May 15 - June 17, 1862
Manassas	August 7 - September 2, 1862
Antietam	September 3-17, 1862
Fredericksburg	November 9 - December 15, 1862
Murfreesboro	December 26, 1862 - January 4, 1863
Chancellorsville	April 27 - May 6, 1863
Gettysburg	June 29 - July 3, 1863
Vicksburg	March 29 - July 4, 1863
Chickamauga	August 16 - September 22, 1863
Chattanooga	November 23-27, 1863
Wilderness	May 4-7, 1864
Atlanta	May 7 - September 2, 1864
Spotsylvania	May 8-21, 1864
Cold Harbor	May 22 - June 3, 1864
Petersburg	June 4, 1864 - April 2, 1865
Shenandoah	August 7 - November 28, 1864
Franklin	November 17-30, 1864
Nashville	December 1-16, 1864
Appomattox	April 3-9, 1865

Campaign streamers are inaugurated to prefer honor on units which distinguished themselves in a campaign or battle. The streamers are individually lettered and are attached to the top of the unit's flag pole.

Negley to fall back on the main body of XIV Corps at Stevens's Gap. Hill had been ordered to attack only when he heard Hindman's artillery, and therefore failed to intervene even as Negley fell back.

The Confederate Plan: Defeat Rosecrans in Detail

Bragg still intended to defeat Rosecrans's forces in detail. He decided to turn his attention to Crittenden's XXI Corps, which had Major General Thomas John Wood's division at Lee and Gordon's Mills, and the other two divisions at Reed's Bridge and Ringgold. This disposition was based on false information about Bragg's dispositions, and when he learned the true disposition on September 12, Crittenden concentrated his corps behind Wood's division. The following day, Bragg, believing that Crittenden's corps was still divided, ordered Polk to coordinate an attack on Wood's division by his own and Walker's corps. Polk later informed Bragg that Crittenden had concentrated, but was ordered to attack without delay as Bragg came up with Buckner's corps.

Despite the fact that he had a superiority of four divisions to three, with two more in imminent prospect once Buckner arrived, Polk did not attack as ordered. By the time Bragg arrived to take local control, it was too late. Crittenden had fallen back.

In the type of campaign that Bragg was trying to wage, speed was of the essence. As a result of his subordinates' caution, he had now lost two excellent opportunities to strike decisive blows at Rosecrans's widely divided army. Rosecrans was becoming aware of Bragg's real dispositions, and he finally began to concentrate his own forces. By September 17, McCook's XX Corps had moved to Stevens's Gap, Thomas's XIV Corps was around Pond Spring in the valley of West Chickamauga Creek southeast of Missionary Ridge, Crittenden's XX Corps was in the area of Lee and Gordon's Mills, and Granger's Reserve Corps had moved into the area of Chattanooga and Rossville. This greatly reduced Bragg's chances to defeat in detail the Army of the Cumberland, especially as the cavalry corps, now commanded by Brigadier General Robert Byington Mitchell (Stanley was sick), had been redeployed to provide effective reconnaissance.

Last Confederate Chance

Despite the fact that his lines of communication would be exposed, Bragg decided that one last chance remained to strike at a portion of the Army of the Cumberland before Rosecrans had completed his concentration. On September 18, the first three brigades from Longstreet's corps arrived. Two more, and Longstreet himself, were due on the following day, and the other four plus the artillery two days later still. Bragg had also received three more brigades from

Mississippi under Brigadier General Bushrod Rust Johnson. On September 18 he decided to attack Crittenden's left wing with the intention of taking McFarland's Gap and Rossville, so cutting Rosecrans's line of communications with Chattanooga. Bragg's chances would have been higher on September 13, when Crittenden could not have called for support, or after September 21, when all of Longstreet's corps would have been at his disposal.

Bragg's scheme called for the corps of Hood (supported by Johnson), Walker, and Buckner to cross West Chickamauga Creek at Reed's Bridge, Alexander's Bridge, and Tedford's Ford respectively to fall on Crittenden's right near Viniard's. Hill's corps was to hold the northern end of McClemore's Cove to prevent any northward advance by the Federal corps of Thomas and McCook, and Polk's corps was to cross the creek at Lee and Gordon's Mills.

The Federal cavalry fought an excellent series of delaying actions, which, combined with the poor roads prevented the three northern Confederate corps from completing their crossing of the creek until the night of September 18/19. The two southern corps reached the creek at nightfall.

Rosecrans guessed Bragg's intention during the morning and ordered Thomas and McCook to head north immediately. During the night, Thomas's corps began to reach the rear of Crittenden's position at about the time that Hill's corps, which had been instructed to prevent the Federal movement, reached the creek too late to intervene.

By dawn on September 19, three of Thomas's four divisions were deployed to hold the high ground beyond Crittenden's left wing, while the fourth shielded Crittenden's right flank. The Confederate corps of Hood and Walker were already across the creek. They were soon joined by Buckner's corps and Major General Benjamin Franklin Cheatham's division of Polk's corps, the latter as a reserve. Thus the scene was set for the Battle of Chickamauga, in which a major part was played by each side's lack of detailed information about the other's strengths and dispositions, which had altered considerably during the previous night.

During the morning, Thomas ordered the division of Brigadier General John Milton Brannan to reconnoiter from its present location (on the road two miles north of Lee and Gordon's Mills) toward the creek. The Federal division encountered and pushed back the dismounted cavalry of Forrest, who called on the nearest Confederate infantry units for support. The result was a general engagement as the fighting spread steadily southwest and involved every division of XIV, XX, and XXI Corps. Neither side gained any significant advantage before nightfall.

The Battle of Chickamauga

During the night, the two commanders turned their deployments to take maximum advantage of the difficult terrain. Rosecrans decided on a defensive alignment and Bragg on an offensive disposition. With the arrival of Longstreet during the night, Bragg divided his Army of Tennessee into two wings, giving command of the left wing to Longstreet and the right to Polk. Bragg's plan for September 20 was an attack by the Confederate

Right: The approach to the Battle of Chickamauga.

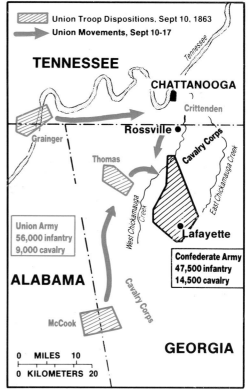

Union Troop Dispositions, Sept 10, 1863
Union Movements, Sept 10-17

TENNESSEE

CHATTANOOGA

Crittenden

Rossville

Grainger

Thomas

Cavalry Corps

East Chickamauga Creek

West Chickamauga Creek

Union Army
56,000 infantry
9,000 cavalry

Lafayette

Confederate Army
47,500 infantry
14,500 cavalry

ALABAMA

Cavalry Corps

McCook

GEORGIA

0   MILES   10
0   KILOMETERS   20

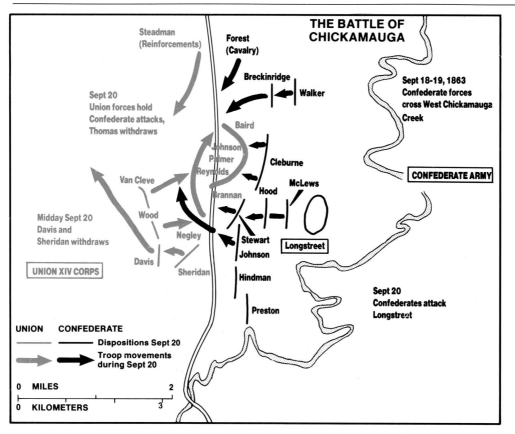

THE BATTLE OF CHICKAMAUGA

Steadman
(Reinforcements)

Forest
(Cavalry)

Breckinridge — Walker

Sept 20
Union forces hold
Confederate attacks,
Thomas withdraws

Baird

Johnson
Palmer
Reynolds

Van Cleve

Cleburne

Hood   McLews

Brannan

Midday Sept 20
Davis and
Sheridan withdraws

Wood

Negley

Stewart
Johnson

Longstreet

Davis

UNION XIV CORPS

Sheridan

Hindman

Preston

Sept 18-19, 1863
Confederate forces
cross West Chickamauga
Creek

CONFEDERATE ARMY

Sept 20
Confederates attack
Longstreet

UNION   CONFEDERATE

——— ——— Dispositions Sept 20

→ → Troop movements
during Sept 20

0 MILES   2

0 KILOMETERS   3

The Battle of
Chickamauga.

forces in a cadenced sequence from north to south, starting at 9:30 a.m. with Major General John Cabell Breckinridge's division. For two hours, the Federal left wing checked the attacks of Polk's formations. Then Rosecrans, misunderstanding the real rather than planned disposition of his forces, made a fatal error.

Wood's division was supposed to be in reserve behind the Federal right wing, but had earlier moved into the line to relieve Negley's division. It was supposed to be in reserve, but had already moved to reinforce the left wing. Rosecrans now tried to strengthen his right wing, where Longstreet's wing was beginning to make significant forward progress, and ordered Wood "to close up and support" Major General Joseph Jones Reynolds's division. Rosecrans thought that Wood would move forward to a position on Reynolds's right flank, but Brannan's division was already located there. Wood moved out of the line and, passing behind Brannan's division, moved back into the line between Brannan's and Reynolds's divisions.

At this point, a column of three Confederate divisions hit the Federal line where Wood's division had been, found no opposition, and pressed ahead through the void on the Federal right wing. Two of McCook's divisions were moving to fill the gap, but reached the scene too late and, being separated from Rosecrans's main force by a total of five Confederate divisions, fell back toward Rossville via McFarland's Gap.

Rosecrans thought that all was lost and joined the retreating divisions. Rosecrans was soon joined by McCook and Crittenden, leaving Thomas in field command by 1:00 p.m. Thomas soon received orders from Rosecrans to pull what forces he could back to Rossville.

Meanwhile, Granger was at McAfee's Church north of the battlefield. Hearing the sound of artillery fire, he decided on his own initiative to support Thomas with Brigadier General James Blair Steedman's division from his Reserve Corps. Steedman's division arrived on the battlefield at 2:30 p.m. and fell in on the right flank of Brannan's division, which was about to be outflanked by the left wing of Longstreet's corps. Thomas managed to repulse two more Confederate outflanking attempts

Lee & Gordon's Mills was a key point in the Battle of Chickamauga, seen here before the battle.

(one on his left and the other on his right) before nightfall. During the night, Thomas managed to withdraw to Rossville with the aid of the two divisions from McCook's corps, which returned from Rossville to the battlefield at about 7:00 p.m. Bragg failed to launch an immediate pursuit, and the Battle of Chickamauga was over.

Chickamauga: the Consequences

The Army of the Cumberland lost three divisions as cohesive formations, and of the 58,225 of its men involved, 16,170 became casualties (1,657 killed, 9,756 wounded, and 4,757 missing). The Army of Tennessee deployed 66,635 men in the battle, and suffered 18,454 casualties (2,312 killed, 14,674 wounded, and 1,468 missing).

The Battle of Chickamauga was a serious defeat for the Union. It could have been a complete disaster, except for the sterling leadership of Thomas in the later stages of the fighting. On the Confederate side, Forrest was the only one to appreciate from the start that Bragg's refusal to launch a pursuit could have dire consequences. Bragg made the senseless error of not maintaining a true reserve and therefore lacked the formation with which to undertake an immediate pursuit.

By the night of September 21, the Army of the Cumberland had pulled back into Chattanooga. Rosecrans was so dispirited that he seemed to accept a Confederate siege as inevitable and ordered the strengthening of the fortifications built by the Confederates. The overall position was now a neat reversal of the situation in mid-August, though Rosecrans maintained a link with the north by means of the bridgehead at Bridgeport, now held by a cavalry division, which was linked to Chattanooga by a cavalry cordon also designed to warn of any Confederate move toward an invasion of Tennessee.

Bragg's Options

Bragg had three possible courses of action. He could turn Rosecrans's position by crossing the Tennessee River either

Known later as "The Rock of Chickamauga," George Henry Thomas was one of the few Federal generals to emerge from the Battle of Chickamauga with an enhanced reputation. Born in Virginia in 1816, Thomas graduated from the U.S. Military Academy in 1840 and joined the artillery. He undertook garrison and frontier duties, distinguished himself in the Mexican War, and rose steadily if unspectacularly in the Federal ranks in the first half of the Civil War. After Chickamauga, he was promoted to command the Army of the Cumberland. He remained in the army after the Civil War, and died during 1870 on active duty as commander of the Division of the Pacific.

upstream or downstream of Chattanooga. He could leave a small covering force outside Chattanooga while he led his main strength to Knoxville in an effort to destroy Burnside's Army of the Ohio. Or he could take Chattanooga under formal siege. The Confederate commander chose the last course.

As a first move, while his infantry completed the Confederate investment of the city on October 1, Bragg sent Wheeler's cavalry to cut Rosecrans's communications in Tennessee. The corps crossed the Tennessee River, advanced to Anderson's, where it burned 300 wagons and captured 1,800 mules, and then headed for Murfreesboro. But Rosecrans's cavalry was snapping at Wheeler's heels, and he was fortunate to return to the Confederate lines on October 8 with his corps no more than demoralized and slightly reduced in strength. The weather was more effective than Wheeler in disrupting Rosecrans's communications, and the Army of the Cumberland's artillery horses died of starvation before the supply line from Bridgeport was reopened on October 27.

Federal reaction

Washington had finally woken up to the fact that a major Federal field army was trapped and in imminent danger of destruction. The first and most obvious response was to strengthen the Army of the Cumberland. As the Army of the Potomac was currently inactive, its XI and XII Corps were detached west. Under Hooker's command, these 20,000 men, 10 batteries of artillery, and 3,000 horses

Pontoons were vital to the operations of both sides in the Civil War, for the first task of a retreating army was to destroy all bridges that could be used by the pursuing enemy. These Federal troops are practicing a river crossing with a piece of artillery in a ''boat'' made of pontoons lashed together and covered with a log deck.

and mules reached Louisville, Kentucky, on October 4 to safeguard the railroad to the southwest and pushed forward to support the Army of the Cumberland. At much the same time, Sherman moved from Mississippi toward Chattanooga with a force of 17,000 men.

Lincoln and the military authorities in Washington also decided that a unified command was necessary in the west. The command inevitably went to Grant, who assumed control of all Federal forces between the Mississippi River and the Allegheny Mountains with the exception of Banks's Army of the Gulf. Given a choice between Thomas or Rosecrans as his subordinate in Chattanooga, Grant chose Thomas. Thomas assumed command on October 19 and received orders from Grant that Chattanooga must be

held at all costs. Grant himself arrived in Chattanooga on October 23.

Other Federal command changes were the appointment of Major General John McAuley Palmer to succeed Thomas at the head of XIV Corps, and the dismissals of McCook and Crittenden, whose corps were amalgamated as the new IV Corps under Granger. The Confederates also made changes. Bragg removed Hill, Polk, and Buckner in favor of Breckinridge, Hardee, and Longstreet.

A plan to reopen land and water communications with Chattanooga from Bridgeport, which had originated under Rosecrans's leadership, was put into action on October 27 as substantial forces had arrived on the north side of the Tennessee River. These forces were the divisions of Howard's XI Corps. Hooker had entrusted protection of the railroad to XII Corps.

The "Cracker Line" Operation

XI Corps crossed the river at Bridgeport and started an eastward advance along the railroad toward Chattanooga. At the same time, Brigadier General William Babcock Hazen and 1,500 men drifted downstream from Chattanooga on pontoons to seize a bridgehead on the southern side of the river at Brown's Ferry. Here, a pontoon bridge was quickly built with the aid of the men of Brigadier General John Basil Turchin's brigade. They were supported by the balance of Hazen's brigade, who had crossed the river from Chattanooga and marched over the neck of land to a point opposite Brown's Ferry. This small but important Federal operation was completed by Palmer's division, which crossed the river at Chattanooga and passed along the northern bank to a point opposite Whiteside's on the railroad before recrossing to safeguard Howard's rear. By the evening of October 28, the "cracker line" was open and supplies were flowing into Chattanooga to supplement those delivered by riverboat.

Bragg did not properly appreciate the significance of this small operation in boosting the morale of the army of the Cumberland and rebuilding its strength. After a desultory shelling of Brown's Ferry and an unsuccessful night attack by four brigades, Bragg felt his position was strong enough to detach Longstreet's corps to tackle Burnside around Knoxville. This reduced Confederate strength to about 40,000, at about the time the Federal strength was boosted by the arrival of Sherman's force.

Sherman Arrives Near Chattanooga

At the head of XV and XVII Corps, Sherman had left Memphis, Tennessee, late in September. Halleck had insisted that he repair the railroad line between Memphis and Decatur as he moved, so progress was slow. Grant then counter-

November 1863, a Union army lay besieged inside Chattanooga, Tennessee. The men were discouraged and hungry. Some tried to desert:

Chattanooga, Tennessee, Friday, November 13, 1863.

Weather warm and pleasant. Our brigade was called to witness the execution of two soldiers for the crime of desertion. The brigade was all in readiness, and formed three sides of a hollow square, along a deep fill in the railroad; then came the procession, headed by the provost marshal, Captain Carroll; following came twelve guards; then came the eight soldiers carrying the coffins of the unfortunate men on their shoulders; then following behind each coffin was the man whose body would soon be placed therein. They moved around so that we might all get to see them, the rear guard closing up. After moving to the center of the square, the coffins were set down on the ground, each man sitting on his coffin; the squad that was to fire the volley took position about ten paces to the front. The ministers spent a few moments with the condemned men, placing bandages over their eyes, and then at the wave of a white handkerchief the volley was discharged, and each man fell off his coffin, dead. We then marched by them to camp, and were dismissed.

manded Halleck's instruction, and Sherman reached Bridgeport on November 15. Grant now disposed of some 60,000 men in Thomas's Army of the Cumberland, two corps of Sherman's Army of the Tennessee, and two corps of the Army of the Potomac under Hooker. Grant decided on an immediate offensive to clear the Confederates from Missionary Ridge.

The plan demanded that Sherman move by land from Bridgeport to Brown's Ferry, where he was to cross to the northern side of the Tennessee River. Sherman was then to move along the river's northern bank to a point opposite

Colt Model 1849 Pocket Pistol

Known as the Baby Dragoon, this weapon, with a five-chamber cylinder, succeeded 15,000 Model 1848 Pocket Pistols. It was a 0·31-inch caliber weapon with a percussion-cap, and production was greater than that of any other Colt pistol: 325,000 in the U.S. and 11,000 in Britain. It had a five- or six-chamber cylinder and was available with a 3-, 4-, 5- or 6-inch barrel. It weighed about 1 lb. 6 oz. with the 5-inch barrel. The weapon was not adopted as standard government issue, but was nevertheless widely used during the Civil War. This is a presentation model delivered to Tsar Nicholas I of Russia.

the outflow of Chickamauga Creek into the Tennessee, cross the river once more, and take Tunnel Hill on the exposed flank of the Confederate forces along Missionary Ridge. Sherman's force would then link up with Thomas's most northerly forces in an advance southwest along the ridge.

Sherman's approach march was delayed by rain, and when his force was finally assembled in its assault area on November 23, it lacked one division that had been stranded on the southern side when the pontoon bridge at Brown's Ferry was swept away. This forced Grant to revise his overall plan. Brigadier General Peter Joseph Osterhaus's stranded division was allocated to Hooker, who was now to take the offensive rather than remain on the defensive to protect the Federal position from any Confederate move down the valley of Lookout Creek.

By this time, the authorities in Washington were becoming concerned about Longstreet's advance against Burnside in Knoxville, and Grant felt forced to order a preliminary attack in an effort to push Bragg into recalling Longstreet. On November 23, Thomas

started a reconnaissance in force toward Orchard Knob and Indian Hill, positions halfway between his Chattanooga positions and the main Confederate line on Missionary Ridge. The attack was surprisingly successful, and Thomas occupied a new forward position including Orchard Knob and Indian Hill.

As a result, Bragg abandoned his plan to send further reinforcements to Longstreet. He moved one division from Lookout Mountain on his left wing to strengthen his right wing in the area immediately to the southwest of Tunnel Hill.

Limited Federal Success at Lookout Mountain

On November 24, Hooker's three divisions attacked the four divisions of Breckinridge's corps in the Lookout Mountain position (two divisions on the western side of the mountain, and two on the neck of lower land separating the mountain from the Tennessee River). Making his main effort on the low defile which the Confederates had failed to fortify, Hooker made rapid progress, but had to halt at 3:00 p.m. because of ammunition shortages and the arrival of thick fog. Bragg appreciated the danger offered by Hooker's advance; during the night, he pulled back his forces south of Chattanooga to Missionary Ridge with a cordon defense of two divisions in forward positions along Chattanooga Creek.

As Hooker attacked on November 24, Sherman began to throw a pontoon bridge across the Tennessee River using equipment stockpiled secretly on the north bank by a division of XIV Corps that had been awaiting his arrival. The Federal bridgehead was expanded steadily, but it was afternoon before Sherman was ready to advance on Tunnel Hill, where defense had been extended farther north by the arrival of another Confederate division diverted to bolster Longstreet.

A Double Envelopment is Planned

Grant now changed his plan to a double envelopment of the Confederates on Missionary Ridge. Sherman would move from the northeast and Hooker from the southwest supplemented, once he had reached the southern end of Missionary Ridge, by an eastward drive by Thomas's forces from their Orchard Knob and Indian Hill positions.

The Battle of Missionary Ridge

Though he was soon reinforced by Howard's XI Corps, Sherman was unable to break the resistance of Major General Patrick Ronayne Cleburne's division on the northern end of Missionary Ridge. Hooker's progress was also slow, for his formations were delayed by the Confederate destruction of the bridges over Chattanooga Creek. Grant, concerned about the lack of progress at the ends of his attack, was even more worried by indications that Bragg was about to reinforce the northern end of Missionary Ridge still further. Grant therefore ordered Thomas to attack the lowest of the three Confederate trench lines on Missionary Ridge. The men of the Army of the Cumberland responded to the demand with great determination and soon took

A great moment of the Civil War was the speech delivered by Abraham Lincoln on November 19, 1863, at the dedication of the national cemetery outside Gettysburg. The impact of the Gettysburg Address at the time was small, but the five-minute speech gained currency and impact as it was quoted in newspapers all over the country. It is now thought to be one of the great speeches of history.

their objective. Moreover, as they were under fire from the two lines higher up the ridge, they swept on forward and took them also, much to the surprise of most Federal commanders who had considered the Army of the Cumberland to have been effectively destroyed by the fighting at Chickamauga. By 4:30 p.m., the Army of Tennessee had broken and started to flee in panic.

Grant did not launch an immediate pursuit. When he pushed divisions forward the following day, they were checked by a single Confederate division that bought the time for Bragg to fall back into Georgia and regroup.

Between November 23 and 25, the Federal side had deployed 56,360 men and suffered losses of 5,824 (753 killed, 4,722 wounded, and 349 missing), while the Confederate side had used 64,165 men and suffered losses of 6,667 (361

killed, 2,160 wounded, and 4,146 missing). Casualties were not disastrously high on either side, but the loss of Chattanooga was an enormous strategic defeat for the Confederacy, as well as a significant blow to Confederate morale. With the city, the Confederacy's main east/west line of communications in the northern sector of the war area was lost, and the Union had pierced the mountain barrier upon which the Confederacy had pinned its northern defense. Just as importantly, Chattanooga was the springboard needed by the Federal side for a decisive thrust deep into the Confederate heartlands the following year.

Unified Command Under Grant

From the beginning of the Civil War to their defeat of Bragg's Army of Tennessee

The Battle of Missionary Ridge on November 25, 1863, sealed the defeat of Bragg's Confederate army outside Chattanooga. At the same time, and in a single stroke, it reconfirmed the fighting skill and determination of Thomas's Army of the Cumberland, which had little regard from Grant when he arrived to take command in this sector.

General Grant took command. He decided to fight his way out of Chattanooga. To do this, he had to capture Missionary Ridge. Three lines of imposing trenches sheltered the Confederates defending the ridge. Grant's plan called for a charge on the first trench at the foot of the ridge. General Phil Sheridan led one of the attacking units at the Battle of Missionary Ridge, 25 November, 1863:

Placing myself in front of Harker's brigade, between the line of battle and the skirmishers, accompanied by only an orderly so as not to attract the enemy's fire, we moved out. Under a terrible storm of shot and shell the line pressed forward steadily through the timber, and as it emerged on the plain took the double-quick and with fixed bayonets rushed at the enemy's first line. Not a shot was fired from our line of battle, and as it gained on my skirmishers they melted into and became one with it, and all three of my brigades went over the rifle-pits simultaneously. They then lay down on the face of the ridge, for a breathing-spell and for protection from the terrible fire of canister and musketry pouring over us from the guns on the crest. At the rifle-pits there had been little use for the bayonet, for most of the Confederate troops, disconcerted by the sudden rush, lay close in the ditch and surrendered, though some few fled up the slope to the next line.

A Confederate general defending the trenches describes what he saw:

''*When the enemy had arrived within about 200 yards our men gave their volley, and a well-directed and fatal one it proved, but then followed a scene of confusion rarely witnessed, and only equalled at a later hour on that day. The order had been issued to retire, but many did not hear it, owing to the reports of their own pieces and the deafening roar of artillery. Others supposed their comrades flying and refused to do likewise. Some feared to retire up the hill, exposed to a heavy fire in their rear, feeling certain, as their movements must be slow, that they would be killed or wounded before reaching their friends above. All order was lost, and each striving to save himself took the shortest direction for the summit. The enemy seeing the confusion*

and retreat moved up their first line at a double quick and came over the breastworks, but I could see some of our brave fellows firing into the enemy's faces and at last falling over-powered ...
''*The troops from below at last reached the works exhausted and breathless, the greater portion so demoralized that they rushed to the rear to place the ridge itself between them and the enemy. It required the utmost efforts of myself and other officers to prevent this, which we finally succeeded in doing. Many fell, broken down from over-exertion, and became deathly sick or fainted. I noticed some instances of slight hemorrhage, and it was fifteen minutes before the nervous systems of those men were so restored as to be able to draw a trigger with steadiness.*''

When the Union soldiers captured this first line they found it terribly exposed to fire from the two trenches further upslope. Without orders they continued up the ridge. When Grant saw this movement he said to his generals: ''Who ordered those men up the hill?'' When the generals denied giving the orders, Grant concluded: ''Some one will suffer for it, if it turns out badly.''

Sheridan continues:

In the meantime Harker's and F.T. Sherman's troops were approaching the partial line of works midway of the ridge, and as I returned to the center of their rear, they were being led by many stands of regimental colors. There seemed to be a rivalry as to which color should be farthest to the front; first one would go forward a few feet, then another would come up to it, the color-bearers vying with one another as to who should be foremost, until finally every standard was planted on the intermediate works. The enemy's fire from the crest during the ascent was terrific in the noise made, but as it was plunging, it over shot and had little effect on those above the second line of pits, but was very uncomfortable for those below, so I deemed it advisable to seek another place, and Wagner's brigade having reassembled and again pressed up the ridge,

I rode up the face to join my troops.

As soon as the men saw me, they surged forward and went over the works on the crest. The parapet of the intrenchment was too high for my horse to jump, so, riding a short distance to the left, I entered through a low place in the line. A few Confederates were found inside, but they turned the butts of their muskets toward me in token of surrender, for our men were now passing beyond them on both their flanks.

The right and right center of my division gained the summit first, they being partially sheltered by a depression in the face of the ridge, the Confederates in their immediate front fleeing down the southern face. When I crossed the rifle-pits on the top the Confederates were still holding fast at Bragg's headquarters, and a battery located there opened fire along the crest, making things most uncomfortably hot. Seeing the danger to which I was exposed, for I was mounted, Colonel Joseph Conrad, of the Fifteenth Missouri, ran up and begged me to dismount. I accepted his excellent advice, and it probably saved my life, but poor Conrad was punished for his solicitude by being seriously wounded in the thigh at the moment he was thus contributing to my safety.

Wildly cheering, the men advanced along the ridge toward Bragg's headquarters, and soon drove the Confederates from this last position capturing a number of prisoners and the battery that had made such stout resistance on the crest - two guns which were named ''Lady Breckenridge'' and ''Lady Buckner'' - General Bragg himself having barely time to escape before his headquarters were taken.

It had been a great Union victory, won by soldiers taking matters into their own hands.

This photograph of Washington, D.C., taken in July 1863, shows the statue of George Washington next to the capital whose dome was still uncompleted. Life in the capitol appears to be unconcerned with the war.

outside Chattanooga, the Federal forces had fought under individual commanders in separate theaters of war. There had been major successes, but the Federal cause was hampered by lack of a single overall commander able to plan and execute a unified strategy that would use all the power of Federal land and naval forces to crush the armed strength of the Confederacy. 1864 would be a presidential election year, and Lincoln was concerned that there was a small but growing minority in the north that called for peace with the Confederacy.

Lincoln had acted almost as his own general in chief since the removal of Major General George Brinton McClellan early in 1862 and his replacement by Halleck. Since that time, the Confederate army had held the Federal army in check in the cockpit of northern Virginia. The string of Federal victories in the western theater could not be exploited fully until the communications center at Nashville had been made completely safe by the elimination of the elusive Confederate armies in the west. Finally, the Federal victories at Gettysburg and Vicksburg, won within a day of each other but separated by 900 miles, highlighted their individual natures and emphasized the need for an overall strategy.

Once he had cleared the Mississippi River, Grant wrote to Washington about the possibilities now open to the Federal forces in the western theater. As a first step, Grant called for the consolidation of the various western departments so that their individual armies could be coordinated effectively. Once this had been achieved, Grant proposed to isolate the Confederate area west of the line between Chattanooga and Mobile, via Atlanta, and Montgomery. This isolation was to be achieved by a "massive rear attack" involving a two-part offensive from south and north. In the south, the forces of Banks's Department of the Gulf and his own Department of the Tennessee, supported by the U.S. Navy, would capture Mobile and advance up the Alabama River to Montgomery. In the north, the forces of Rosecrans's Department of the Cumberland would drive through Chattanooga to Atlanta. All the

Confederate forces trapped to the west of this Federal cordon would then be isolated and destroyed.

Lincoln felt that Grant's plan was basically sound, but felt that political considerations demanded a delay in Grant's plans for the Mobile to Montgomery axis. Instead, Banks's department was ordered to demonstrate up the Red River toward Shreveport, near the Louisiana/Texas boundary, to emphasize Federal strength to the French interlopers of Napoleon III in Mexico. For this reason, the Department of the Gulf was left out of the consolidation of other western departments under Grant in October 1863. Early in the winter of 1863, Grant prepared the victors of Chattanooga for an advance on Atlanta in the spring of 1864, but again urged Lincoln to authorize his Mobile expedition. Lincoln again refused and instructed Grant to

Used in the fortifications of Atlanta, the 12-pounder Napoleon was the standard piece of artillery used by both sides in the Civil War. It was a smoothbore muzzleloading piece of field artillery with a caliber of 4·62 inches. The barrel was made of bronze, though Confederate copies cast during the war were made of iron with a reinforced breech. It had a maximum effective range of between 800 and 1,000 yards.

provide proposals for a Federal grand offensive in the spring of 1864.

Grant Conceives a Decisive Strategy

In January 1864, Grant responded with a plan for a four-pronged offensive. Of the four major armies involved, the first was to advance on Atlanta. The second would take Mobile using forces freed by Banks's planned capture of Shreveport, while the third drove across the center of North Carolina between New Bern and Greensboro to cut Lee's lines of communication with the south. The fourth would take the offensive against the Army of Northern Virginia with the intention of finally defeating it in open battle.

Lincoln, aware that Lee had always wished to capture the large quantities of military supplies in the Washington area, turned down the North Carolina part of Grant's plan; it would have weakened the defense of Washington by 60,000 men.

In February 1864, Congress revived the rank of lieutenant general, and on March 9 Grant was elevated to this rank in recognition of his victories in the west. Lincoln then replaced Halleck with Grant as general-in-chief. Once Grant reached Washington, Lincoln, Stanton, and Grant used the rest of March to establish a new high command system. Lincoln and Stanton handed over to the new general-in-chief several important command, staff, and communications functions. Stanton was so impressed with Grant's capabilities and intentions that he warned his general staff bureau chiefs to make sure they met Grant's requirements and schedules.

To help guarantee his relative freedom from interference from Washington, Grant established his headquarters outside the capital in northern Virginia, keeping effective control of his subordinate commands by means of a vast telegraph network. Grant had overall command of

Artillery in the Confederate earthworks outside Atlanta during 1864.

77

Known as "Little Phil" as he was only 5 feet 5 inches tall, Phil Henry Sheridan was the only senior Federal cavalry commander who matched the excellence of his Confederate counterparts. Where Sheridan scored over the Confederate cavalrymen, however, was in the complete nature of his leadership skills, which were comprehensively proved by his Shenandoah Valley campaign between August 1864 and March 1865. Born in New York in 1831, Sheridan graduated from the U.S. Military Academy in 1853, and then served in the infantry and cavalry. Sheridan was only a lieutenant at the beginning of the Civil War; after filling a number of administrative positions, he received his first command as colonel of the 2nd Michigan Cavalry in May 1862. Thereafter, his rise was rapid. Sheridan remained in the army after the Civil War, succeeding Sherman as commanding general in 1884. He died in 1888, just a few months after becoming a full general.

four military divisions totaling 17 sub-commands and 500,000 soldiers. In Washington, there was a war room controlled by Halleck, now designated Chief of Staff, U.S. Army, for filtering incoming information, thereby saving Grant the task of reading irrelevant material. Another substantial portion of Grant's overall burden was borne by Brigadier General Montgomery Cunningham Meigs, the Quartermaster General.

Federal Success in the East

Grant spent much of his time with the Army of the Potomac in the angle of the Rappahannock and Rapidan rivers west of Fredericksburg, but he devoted much of April 1864 to finalizing his plan for the annihilation of the Confederacy's armed strength. The general-in-chief's grand strategic plan drew on the advantages offered by his own victories in the west and eventually fixed on a large, concentrated effort in which the Federal armies, aided by the U.S. Navy where appropriate, would drive toward a common center deep in the Confederacy.

Within this overall ambition, Grant planned to deny the Confederates their interior lines of communication. In overall terms, Grant's plan had several objectives. One was to maneuver Lee and the

Philip Henry Sheridan

For further references see pages 60, 74, 82, 85, *92*, 96, *98, 100, 115,* 124, 125, 129

The Federal advance on Richmond in May and June 1864 was a carefully planned offensive with large numbers of well trained and well equipped troops, but Grant was unable to get past the wily Lee and bring the Civil War to the anticipated swift conclusion.

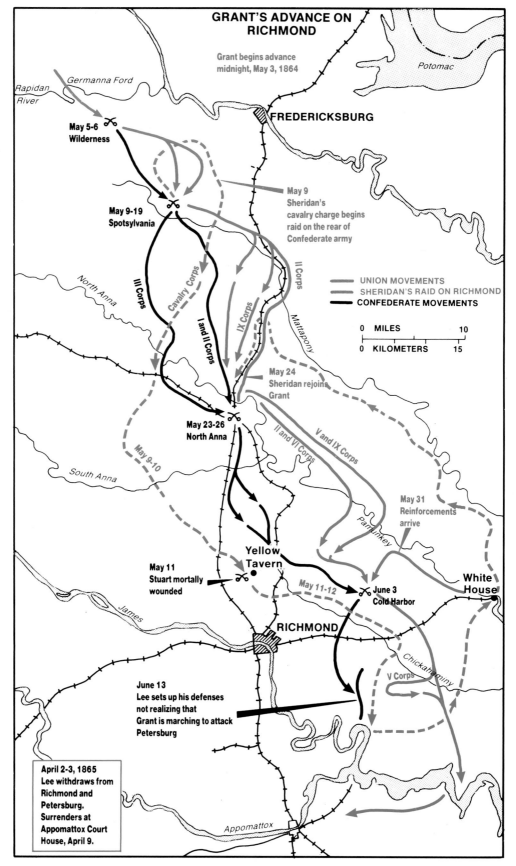

GRANT'S ADVANCE ON RICHMOND

Grant begins advance midnight, May 3, 1864

Potomac

Rapidan River

Germanna Ford

FREDERICKSBURG

May 5-6 Wilderness

May 9 Sheridan's cavalry charge begins raid on the rear of Confederate army

May 9-19 Spotsylvania

North Anna

II Corps

Mattapony

II Corps

Cavalry Corps

I and II Corps

IX Corps

UNION MOVEMENTS
SHERIDAN'S RAID ON RICHMOND
CONFEDERATE MOVEMENTS

| 0 | MILES | 10 |
| 0 | KILOMETERS | 15 |

May 24 Sheridan rejoins Grant

May 23-26 North Anna

II and VI Corps

V and IX Corps

May 9-10

South Anna

Pamunkey

May 31 Reinforcements arrive

James

May 11 Stuart mortally wounded

Yellow Tavern

May 11-12

June 3 Cold Harbor

White House

RICHMOND

V Corps

Chickahominy

June 13 Lee sets up his defenses not realizing that Grant is marching to attack Petersburg

April 2-3, 1865 Lee withdraws from Richmond and Petersburg. Surrenders at Appomattox Court House, April 9.

Appomattox

Above: The capture of Fort De Russy by Federal forces on March 14, 1864, was the first step in the Federal forces' second campaign in the Red River region of Texas.

Opposite Above: Construction work by men of the Federal Military Telegraph System, a high-quality service run by civilians for the Secretary of War. The system had 12,000 civilian telegraphers and operated over some 15,000 miles of telegraph wires.

Opposite Below: One of the most contentious episodes of the Civil War was the "Fort Pillow Massacre" on April 12, 1864. Federal losses were 231 killed and 226 captured; Confederate losses were 14 killed and 86 wounded.

Army of Northern Virginia away from the Rapidan wilderness so that the Federal forces could defeat them in open country, another to use an army drawn from the Federal garrison forces in various southern seaports to cut the line of the James and Appomattox rivers as a means of denying Lee reinforcement from the south. He also planned to use Sherman for a deep wheeling movement through the south to complete the envelopment of the Confederate forces in the region east of the Mississippi River, and to strike up the Alabama River from Mobile.

By mid-April 1864, Grant had issued orders to the four army commanders involved with his scheme, which envisaged the use of 300,000 Federal soldiers against about 150,000 Confederate troops.

In the eastern theater, the main effort was to be made by Meade's Army of the Potomac together with Burnside's independent IX Corps. Under Grant's personal supervision, this force of 120,000 men was to strike at the Army of Northern Virginia's 63,000 men deployed along the Rapidan River. Two subsidiary efforts were to support the main effort. On the Army of the Potomac's right flank in the

Shenandoah Valley, the 23,000 men of Major General Franz Sigel's Army of West Virginia were to threaten and, if possible, capture Lee's principal rail hub at Lynchburg, Virginia. Farther to the south, the 33,000 men of Major General Benjamin Franklin Butler's Army of the James were entrusted with skirting the southern side of the James River to menace and, if possible, take Richmond and destroy the railroads south of Petersburg, Virginia.

Farther southwest, Sherman had succeeded Grant as head of the Military Division of the Mississippi on March 18. The task of his 100,000 men was to take Atlanta, in the process destroying the resources of central Georgia and eliminating the 65,000-man Army of Tennessee, which had been commanded by Johnston since December 27, 1863, Bragg having been replaced in December 1863 by Hardee and then Polk for short periods.

Still farther to the southwest, Banks was to complete his Red River operation as rapidly as possible and, with the aid of Rear Admiral David Glasgow Farragut's naval forces, make an amphibious assault on Mobile.

On May 4, 1864, Grant's overall strategy to destroy the Confederacy's

military and economic cohesion was put into effect as Meade and Sherman set off on their assigned tasks. The Army of the Potomac, which totaled seven infantry and one cavalry corps, was a leaner and ultimately more effective fighting machine than it had ever been before. The infantry corps each deployed 25,000 men, and Major General Philip Henry Sheridan's cavalry corps had 12,000 men. The Army of Northern Virginia mustered 70,000 men in three infantry and one cavalry corps.

It was the first time that Grant had opposed Lee, and the Federal commander enjoyed the considerable advantages provided by possession of the strategic and tactical initiatives. After crossing the Rapidan River, Grant opted to move past Lee's right wing rather than try to outflank his left wing. This plan offered considerable dangers while the Army of the Potomac crossed Lee's front, but meant he could be supplied from the coast. Otherwise, his army would have to rely on an inadequate railroad network back to Alexandria, Virginia. It would also reduce the hobbling effect of the army's vast transportation force, currently numbering 4,000 wagons and 60,000 animals.

The Battle of The Wilderness

The Army of the Potomac had little room to maneuver and had therefore to cross The Wilderness, where Hooker had come to grief the previous year. The army halted at Chancellorsville to allow its wagon train time to cross the Rapidan River, and Lee struck at the Federal right flank on May 5 in the Battle of The Wilderness. Meade swung his two available corps into line against Lee's two corps and struck back hard. The desperately hard fighting in the tangled confines of this inhospitable region, where artillery could not be brought to bear and the infantry had to bear the brunt of the combat, continued until May 1. So intense was the fighting and so dry the conditions that part of The Wilderness caught fire, and considerable numbers of wounded men burned to death before they could escape. On May 6, Lee attacked again, and Longstreet's corps arrived as usual in

The Battle of The Wilderness was fought between May 5 and 7, 1864. It was the first of several major battles between Meade's Army of the Potomac and Lee's Army of Northern Virginia as the Federal forces under Grant's overall command advanced on the Confederate capital of Richmond, Virginia. Grant's plan was to operate against Lee's army wherever it might be found with the intention of finding and outflanking the Confederate right as he drove on Richmond. In the Battle of The Wilderness, the two armies met as the Army of the Potomac was still tangled in the tangles of The Wilderness, an area 14 miles long by 10 miles wide. The fighting of the first day involved two separate, but equally inconclusive, engagements between confused formations. The following day, Grant forced a general engagement that was checked by determined Confederate counterattacks, though Longstreet was wounded near the spot where Jackson had been mortally hit the previous year. At nightfall, the battle was undecided despite the furious fighting of the day. The last day of the battle was spent trying to put out the fires that had been started by the fighting and trying to rescue wounded men trapped in the burning thickets.

Above: The Wilderness battlefield was covered with the underbrush that made it all but impossible for the generals to fight an organized battle.
Left: Despite the Enrollment Act of March 3, 1863, passed to create a structure for drafting men into the Federal army, there was still a considerable effort by individual states to entice volunteers.

Lying on the railroad line from Chattanooga to Atlanta, Resaca was the second point at which Johnston attempted to check Sherman's advance on the Georgia capital. In the Battle of Resaca between May 13 and 16, 1864, the Confederates checked the Federal momentum to the southeast, were threatened by an outflanking movement, and then fell back to Dallas.

perfect order to plunge into the fray and drive the Federals back. Unfortunately, Longstreet was accidentally wounded by his own men and was out of action until October 1864.

The battle favored the Confederates, but was neither won nor lost. The fighting cost the Federals 17,666 men (2,246 killed, 12,073 wounded, and 3,347 missing) out of 101,895 involved, while the Confederates suffered about 7,750 casualties from 61,025 men engaged.

In his first encounter with Lee, Grant had been worsted though not beaten. Under comparable circumstances, Lee's earlier Federal opponents had pulled back to the north. Grant was of a different mettle. He ordered the Army of the Potomac's leading corps to head as rapidly as possible for Spotsylvania to cut into the Confederate line of communication between Lee and Richmond.

Lee was too astute for such a ploy, however, and marched to the same point along parallel roads. Stuart's cavalry

harassed the Army of the Potomac and slowed it just enough for Lee to arrive first and construct earth and log defenses on the commanding heights covering the route to Richmond. Had Meade been able to send Sheridan's cavalry ahead in corps strength, he would in all probability have forestalled Lee, but he had allocated two divisions to protect the already well-protected wagon train in his rear.

Sheridan appealed directly to Grant, who overruled Meade and ordered that the cavalry should be used as a single fighting force. On May 9, Sheridan was sent on a raid designed to draw off Stuart and, if possible, destroy his command. Sheridan performed his task with great skill, fighting the Confederate cavalry in a series of running engagements including the Battle of Yellow Tavern (May 11), where Stuart was mortally wounded. The Federal cavalry threatened Richmond and then raided farther south before returning on May 24 after completing the destruction of Lee's cavalry as an effective fighting force.

The Battle of Spotsylvania

On May 9, the Army of the Potomac struck at the Army of Northern Virginia's road block. The main Battle of Spotsylvania lasted for four days and again ended without a clear victory. The Federal forces twice broke through the Confederate line, but in each case became disorganized and could not exploit their potential advantage in the face of furious counterattacks. There was fighting on other days, but by May 20, Grant had decided that the Confederate position was too strong to be overwhelmed by direct assault. Despite the fact that on May 11 he had written to·Halleck that ''I propose to fight it out on this line if it takes all summer,'' Grant on May 20 again tried to slip past Lee and push south as a means of enveloping Lee's right flank. It is impossible to arrive at any accurate figures for casualties in the Spotsylvania fighting, but it is likely that Federal losses were between 17,000 and 18,000, while those of the Confederates were between 9,000 and 10,000.

Lee, always conscious of the fact that he had considerably smaller forces than Grant, now moved to avoid Grant's planned trap. Rather than challenge the Army of the Potomac in open battle, the Army of Northern Virginia fell back to the line of the North Anna River and dug in just north of Hanover Junction during May 22. Grant arrived the following day, but after three inconclusive days, he

One of the heaviest pieces of artillery used by the Federals in the Civil War was the 13-inch coast mortar known as the ''Dictator.'' Mounted in a reinforced railroad car, this weapon was used in the siege of Petersburg. It weighed 17,000 lb., and with a 20-lb. charge of black powder could hurl its 200-lb. shell a maximum of 4,325 yards. The ''Dictator'' was fired against the Confederate positions around Petersburg by Company G of the 1st Connecticut Heavy Artillery.

A classic photograph of Ulysses S. Grant outside his tent during the Battle of Cold Harbor, which was fought between May 31 and June 12, 1864. On his shoulders, Grant wears the three stars of a lieutenant general.

decided once more that the Confederate position was too strong and moved off to the southeast.

Butler Trapped at Bermuda Hundred

Meanwhile, Butler had pushed his Army of the James up the peninsula toward Richmond, but during May he was outmaneuvered by General Pierre Gustave Toutant Beauregard. By mid-June, he was trapped between the James and Appomattox rivers at Bermuda Hundred. Banks suffered an equal lack of overall success in his Red River expedition and could not even attempt to take Mobile. Butler and Banks were replaced for their failure to execute their parts of Grant's grand strategy, which was thus reduced to two components.

Always moving inside Grant's line of march, Lee arrived in the defenses of Richmond during May 28, and the Army of the Potomac took up position opposite the Army of Northern Virginia two days later. Lee disposed his army along an eight-mile front with its right wing anchored on the Chickahominy River, its center between Cold Harbor and Mechanicsville, and its left wing stretching out as far as Atlee's Station on the Fredericksburg and Potomac Railroad.

The Battle of Cold Harbor

In one of the most poorly conceived moves of his career, Grant decided on an immediate assault on the Confederate positions without proper reconnaissance. On June 3, the Battle of Cold Harbor saw the decimation of three Federal corps in little more than an hour. The repulsed Federal forces did not fall back to their own lines, but dug in close to the Confederate positions and inaugurated a period of primitive trench warfare. Coming at the end of a month-long campaign, Cold Harbor cost the Army of the Potomac about 7,000 casualties and the Army of Northern Virginia about 1,500. The complete campaign had resulted in about 55,000 Federal casualties (some 46 percent of Grant's original strength) and

about 32,000 Confederate casualties (also some 46 percent of Lee's original strength). However, while Grant could replace his casualties in a matter of weeks, Lee could hardly replace his at all.

Grant's next step was a move that was both daring in its concept and skillful in its execution. Between June 12 and 16, the whole of the Army of the Potomac broke off from its positions outside Richmond. While one corps embarked at White House on the York River for movement around the peninsula and up the James River to reinforce the Army of the James at Bermuda Hundred, on the north side of the river, the other four corps and the army's train marched across the front of the Army of Northern Virginia.

Occurring after the Battles of The Wilderness, Spotsylvania, and the North Anna, the Battle of Cold Harbor was the fourth general engagement of Grant's advance toward Richmond. Grant believed that Lee's Army of Northern Virginia was overextended along a six-mile line, so he decided to split the Confederate force. However, the Federal advance was delayed

for 24 hours. Grant's forces were repulsed on June 3 by defenders in a well prepared position. Grant called off the attack after one disastrous hour that cost him 7,000 casualties to Lee's 1,500. The ten-day Cold Harbor episode cost the Army of the Potomac 13,708 casualties out of about 108,000 men; the Army of Northern Virginia lost about 3,000 out of 59,000.

Assembling on the northern side of the James River just downstream of Wilcox's Landing, the bulk of the Army of the Potomac crossed a 2,100-foot pontoon bridge (the longest ever built up to that time) and moved forward to take Petersburg under siege from June 18. A major depot was established at City Point, complete with a railroad to the front, and the siege continued into the following year.

Lee Trapped at Richmond and Petersburg

After 44 days of continuous mobile warfare, Lee was finally committed to posi-tional warfare in a campaign of trenches and siege apparatus controlled, ironically, by two of history's greatest exponents of mobile warfare. Grant sought constantly to find an exposed flank on Lee's right, and Lee constantly countered by modifying his own positions, so the two generals were in effect maneuvering their fortifications rather than their formations! The result was a steady extension of the siege lines from the eastern side of Petersburg around its southeastern side, and then westward out to the line of Gravelly Run, 10 miles southwest of Petersburg.

Once his basic position was fixed, Lee decided that he could afford to reduce his strength by reinforcing Early's corps in

Right: Major General Quincy Adams Gillmore commanded X Corps in Butler's unfortunate James River campaign of May and June 1864. Born in Ohio, Gillmore was a professional soldier and engineer who graduated at the top of his class from West Point in 1849. He remained in the army after the Civil War and died on active duty during 1888 with the rank of colonel.

Below right: The siege of Petersburg in mid-June 1864, before the gradual extension of the siege lines to the south and then around to the west to complete a partial encirclement of this Confederate city.

Opposite top: Federal soldiers in the trenches outside Petersburg.
Opposite Below: ''The Interrupted Game'' shows the alarm in a Federal trench after the arrival of a Confederate mortar shell.

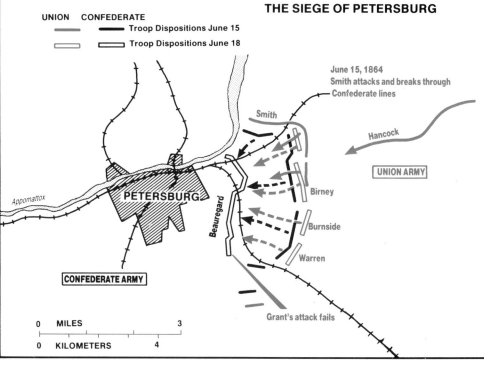

THE SIEGE OF PETERSBURG

UNION   CONFEDERATE

Troop Dispositions June 15

Troop Dispositions June 18

June 15, 1864
Smith attacks and breaks through
Confederate lines

Smith

Hancock

UNION ARMY

PETERSBURG

Appomattox

Beauregard

Birney

Burnside

Warren

CONFEDERATE ARMY

Grant's attack fails

0   MILES   3

0   KILOMETERS   4

the Shenandoah Valley with a view to a raid toward Washington. During the first part of July, Early advanced against the Federal force commanded by Major General David Hunter, who had replaced Sigel. Hunter received confused orders from Halleck and retired up the valley. However, on reaching the Potomac River, Hunter retired westward into the Appalachian Mountains and thereby uncovered Washington to a continued Confederate advance. The opportunity was seized eagerly by Early, who pushed through Maryland and, delayed slightly on July 9 by a Federal force at Frederick, reached the northern outskirts of Washington on July 11. Here, the Confederate force fought an inconclusive skirmish near Fort Stevens. Grant was at City Point when the news of Early's offensive arrived and immediately ordered the embarkation of his VI Corps for

While Grant campaigned outside Petersburg, Sheridan was pursuing his Shenandoah Valley campaign. The campaign destroyed the Confederate force and eliminated the valley's produce as a source of food for the Confederacy.

Left: This illustration of the soldier's rest at Alexandria, Virginia, shows an idealized view of the reception generally given to soldiers in the Civil War.

Below: This Matthew Brady photograph of the between-decks area of a transport steamer probably shows Federal soldiers traveling home on leave after being released from the hospital.

93

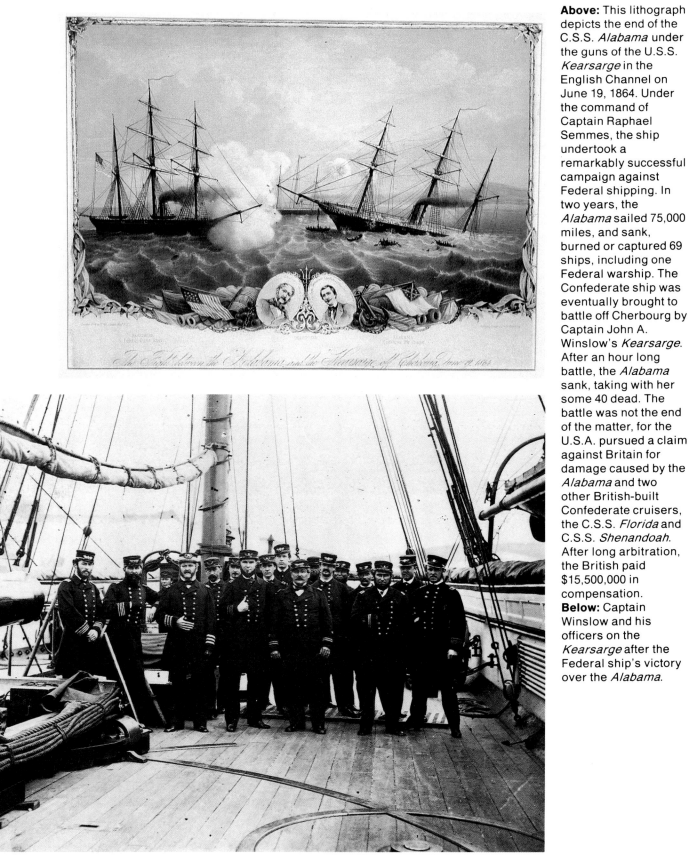

Above: This lithograph depicts the end of the C.S.S. *Alabama* under the guns of the U.S.S. *Kearsarge* in the English Channel on June 19, 1864. Under the command of Captain Raphael Semmes, the ship undertook a remarkably successful campaign against Federal shipping. In two years, the *Alabama* sailed 75,000 miles, and sank, burned or captured 69 ships, including one Federal warship. The Confederate ship was eventually brought to battle off Cherbourg by Captain John A. Winslow's *Kearsarge*. After an hour long battle, the *Alabama* sank, taking with her some 40 dead. The battle was not the end of the matter, for the U.S.A. pursued a claim against Britain for damage caused by the *Alabama* and two other British-built Confederate cruisers, the C.S.S. *Florida* and C.S.S. *Shenandoah*. After long arbitration, the British paid $15,500,000 in compensation.
Below: Captain Winslow and his officers on the *Kearsarge* after the Federal ship's victory over the *Alabama*.

This scene on board the U.S.S. *Hampshire*, a square-rigged warship with auxiliary steam power, emphasizes the size of the muzzleloading guns that were still a major part of the armament of warships in this period. Located to fire broadsides, the guns had modern features such as an elevating screw, but were similar to the weapons of the Napoleonic Wars and the War of 1812 in being based on a massive wooden carriage, with a breeching and two gun tackles. The breeching was a thick rope that passed through the cascable (knob behind the breech) and two eye bolts on the carriage before being attached to the ship's side to limit recoil distance, while the tackles, mounted lower on the carriage's rear, were used to run out the gun after it had been loaded.

waterborne movement to the capital. VI Corps arrived on July 11, and once he realized that elements of the Army of the Potomac were present, Early withdrew on July 12.

Sheridan's Shenandoah Valley Campaign

Grant now saw that the division of the region into four departments had hindered effective action against Early and ordered their amalgamation into the Middle Military Division covering Washington, western Maryland, and the Shenandoah Valley. Despite protests that his nominee was too young, Washington gave command of the new division to Sheridan during August. Sheridan's instructions were to hunt down and destroy Early, which the 33-year-old achieved in a campaign of extraordinary skill characterized by remarkable coordination of his infantry, cavalry, and artillery resources. Sheridan defeated Early at Winchester and Fisher's Hill during September, and destroyed him at Cedar Creek in October. Then, in order to stop further Confederate

raids and to prevent Lee from using the crops of the region to feed the Army of Northern Virginia, Sheridan devastated the valley.

On March 17, Grant had met Sherman in Nashville to discuss his overall strategy for destroying the Confederacy, and Sherman's offensive toward Atlanta within this grand plan.

Like Grant, Sherman now wore two hats. As commanding general of the Division of the Mississippi, Sherman had an administrative role as controller and defender of a huge logistical system that drew on regions as far apart as St. Louis, Louisville, and Cincinnati to concentrate equipment and other supplies in the great base depot at Nashville. In logistical terms, Nashville was as important to the Union in the west as Washington was in the east. A 90-mile railroad, built and operated by soldiers, connected Nashville with the Tennessee River, where a substantial force of river steamers was available for further large-scale movement. Nashville was also connected to Louisville by rail.

Sherman also had a field role as the supervising general of three armies. Sher-

The Federal attack on Fort Fisher, North Carolina, was undertaken on December 25, 1864, by forces of the Army of the James under Major General Benjamin Franklin Butler. The object of the exercise was to take the fort and so prevent Wilmington harbor from being used by the Confederates. After the initial assault, which got to within 75 yards of Fort Fisher, Butler called off the attack because he feared exceptionally heavy casualties.

man was due to receive two of his best divisions back from Banks's Red River expedition during May 1864, and with the backing of his administrative and logistical system, he would then be ready to begin his push on Atlanta. Sherman's tasks were to destroy Johnston's forces and capture Atlanta, which was the Confederacy's second most important industrial center after Richmond. In overall terms, Sherman had 100,000 men and 256 guns in the Army of the Cumberland (under the command of Thomas with three infantry and one cavalry corps), the Army of the Tennessee (under the command of McPherson with three infantry corps), and the Army of the Ohio (under the command of Major General John McAllister Schofield with one infantry corps and one cavalry division).

Defending the approaches to Atlanta

Left: John Adolph Dahlgren was born in 1809, the son of the Swedish consul at Philadelphia. He became a midshipman in the U.S. Navy during 1826, and as an ordnance specialist, he designed the Dahlgren gun, which was widely used in the Civil War. In April 1861, he took command of the Washington Naval Yard, and in July 1862, he was appointed Chief of the Ordnance Bureau.

Below: A Dahlgren gun on board a Federal gunboat on the Mississippi River.

Sheridan at the Battle of Winchester (September 19, 1864), the first of the major Federal successes in Sheridan's Shenandoah Valley campaign of 1864-65. Sheridan's horse, named Rienzi, had been bought as a three-year-old in the spring of 1862 when the general was stationed near Rienzi, Mississippi. The horse stood over 17 hands high and was immensely strong. In October 1864, Sheridan galloped 20 miles from Winchester to the Battle of Cedar Creek on this fine animal. Sheridan then changed the horse's name to Winchester. After its death the horse was stuffed and is now an exhibit in the Smithsonian Institution.

Typical of the many divisional generals who served the Federal cause well during the Civil War was Major General Truman Seymour. A Vermont graduate of the U.S. Military Academy in 1846, Seymour first commanded a division in June 1862 and then took part in many of the battles and coastal campaigns of the eastern theater up to the end of the war. After the war, he chose to remain in the army and, like so many others, had to take a reduction in rank. He retired in 1876 as a major in the 5th Artillery and died in 1891.

Below: Sheridan's celebrated charge at the head of Federal cavalry in the Battle of Winchester.

Sheridan, second from the left, with some of his senior officers in the Shenandoah Valley campaign. On the right is Major General George Custer, on Custer's right is Sheridan's chief of staff, Lieutenant Colonel James Forsyth. Seated in the center is Major General George Crook.

was Johnston's Department of the West, whose 60,000 infantry and 5,000 cavalry were allocated to Johnston's own Army of Tennessee and Polk's single-corps Army of Mississippi.

Sherman's Atlanta Campaign

Sherman moved off on May 4, 1864, the same day that the Army of the Potomac crossed the Rapidan River. Johnston, fully aware of the extent to which his forces were outnumbered, decided to remain on the defensive and so preserve his strength with the twin objective of slowing Sherman's advance as much as possible, and of holding Atlanta. Johnston knew that he could not hope to defeat Sherman, but like an increasing number of the Confederacy's senior commanders, he looked hopefully to the possibility that Lincoln might be defeated in the 1864 presidential election by a candidate prepared to consider peace with the Confederacy.

Sherman's march to Atlanta in the summer of 1864 resulted in the Federal capture of the Confederacy's second most important city, together with its irreplaceable industrial capability.

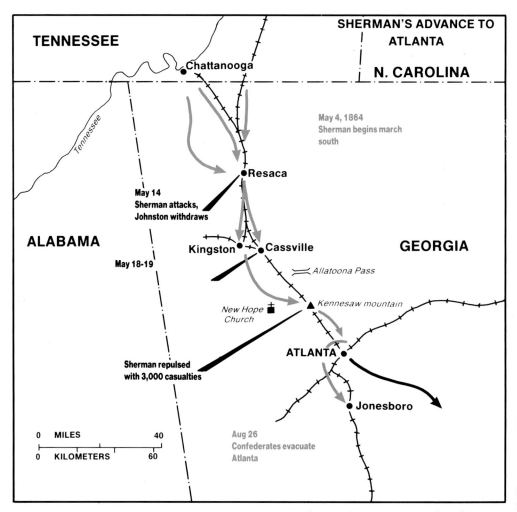

SHERMAN'S ADVANCE TO ATLANTA

TENNESSEE

N. CAROLINA

Chattanooga

Tennessee

May 4, 1864
Sherman begins march
south

Resaca

May 14
Sherman attacks,
Johnston withdraws

ALABAMA

May 18-19

Kingston   Cassville

GEORGIA

Allatoona Pass

New Hope
Church

Kennesaw mountain

Sherman repulsed
with 3,000 casualties

ATLANTA

Jonesboro

0   MILES   40

0   KILOMETERS   60

Aug 26
Confederates evacuate
Atlanta

Between May 4 and mid-July, Sherman's Atlanta campaign mirrored Grant's progress in the eastern theater. There were almost daily fights as Johnston fell back, found a strong defensive position and deployed, Sherman deployed and reconnoitered for an exposed flank, Johnston fell back once more, and Sherman gathered his forces to follow Johnston. Only on June 27, when the muddy conditions prevented any reconnaissance from finding an open flank, did Sherman consider and execute a frontal attack against one of Johnston's prepared positions. This Battle of Kennesaw Mountain was a costly Federal defeat, much like that at Cold Harbor. In the 17,733-man Confederate force, losses totaled 270 killed and wounded as well as 172 missing, while in the 16,225-man Federal force losses totaled 1,999 killed and wounded as well as 52 missing. Sherman learned his lesson. He returned to maneuver, and Johnston once more fell back, this time to positions covering Atlanta.

Johnston's campaign had been remarkably successful. He had forced Sherman to consume 74 precious days in an advance of just 100 miles, and he now occupied strong defensive positions in front of his bastion city with his forces more or less intact. However, the Confederate government was not happy with the campaign fought by Johnston, who was replaced during July by Lieutenant General John Bell Hood. An altogether more aggressive commander, he was, in the circumstances, just what the Confederates did not need.

On July 20, Sherman maneuvered to reach around the northeastern side of Atlanta. Hood launched a large-scale attack, which was beaten off. Hood pulled back into Atlanta. Then, as Sherman prepared to invest Atlanta, Hood

Left: The capture of Lost Mountain on June 17, 1864, was one of the few Federal successes in the otherwise disastrous Battle of Kennesaw Mountain. It took place during the advance on Atlanta and was perhaps the worst tactical battle fought by Sherman, a frontal assault that was beaten back with heavy losses.

Below: This George N. Barnard photograph shows part of the Confederate defenses in front of Atlanta.

Left: Part of the earthworks improvised by Federal forces during the fighting on Kennesaw Mountain.

Below: The Battle of Kennesaw Mountain again revealed the futility of a frontal attack on prepared defenses. 17,733 Confederates suffered only 270 killed and 172 missing, but they beat back a 16,225-man Federal attack and inflicted casualties of 1,999 killed and wounded.

Right: The battlefield at Peach Tree Creek, one of the opening moves in the battle for Atlanta.
Below: Hood made a second attempt to beat the Federal forces advancing on Atlanta in the Battle of Atlanta. Hardee's corps and Wheeler's cavalry division fell on the left flank of McPherson's Army of the Tennessee. McPherson was killed. Despite being outnumbered the Federal soldiers overcame their initial surprise and drove back the Confederates with the loss of 8,000 men for only 3,722 of their own soldiers.

THE MILITARY HISTORY OF THE UNITED STATES

The Battle of Allatoona
on October 5, 1864,
was part of Hood's
counterstroke after the
loss of Atlanta. It
served as a preface to
the Franklin and
Nashville campaign
that began on
November 14. The
860-man Federal
garrison at Allatoona
was entrusted with the
protection of a million
rations of bread for
Sherman's soldiers in
Atlanta. Sherman
realized that a
Confederate effort
might be aimed at this
vital depot, so he
boosted its strength to
1,945 men. They
successfully fought off
a Confederate assault
by divisional strength,
some 2,000 or more
men, inflicting just
under 800 casualties
for the loss of 707 of its
own men.

Left: John Bell Hood was one of the best junior generals of the Confederacy, and he was without equal as a combat leader at brigade and divisional level. Hood was out of his depth when he commanded the Army of Tennessee at Atlanta, however. He married in 1868 at the age of 37, and before he and his wife died of yellow fever in 1878, they had 11 children.
Below: A Matthew Brady photograph of the roundhouse of the Georgia Railroad, destroyed by the Confederates before they abandoned the city.

attacked again, with no greater success. Sherman now tried to cut the Confederates' lines of communication with deep-probing cavalry raids, but they too gained no real success.

Hood Abandons Atlanta

Realizing that the defenses of Atlanta were too strong for his comparatively small forces, Sherman now planned a deep envelopment of the Confederate left using virtually his complete strength on August 31. Though Hood was at first convinced that Sherman was retreating, he then realized that his final position was about to be cut off. He lacked any real means for an offensive as he had wasted his meager reserve strength in the previous attacks. After the failure of Hardee's corps to halt the Federal advance at Jonesboro, south of Atlanta,

Piled high with the household goods of refugees, the last Confederate train prepares to leave Atlanta before the arrival of the Federal army.

Hood abandoned the city and took his surviving forces by back roads to link up with Hardee south of Jonesboro.

Sherman signaled to Lincoln from Atlanta that "Atlanta is ours and fairly won." The campaign so far had cost 21,656 Federal and 27,565 Confederate casualties. The Federal strength could be restored without delay; the Confederate losses were permanent.

The Battle of Mobile Bay

The capture of Atlanta was a great fillip to Lincoln in the 1864 election, as was the Federal victory in the naval Battle of Mobile Bay on August 5, 1864. Here, Admiral Farragut led a Federal squadron of four ironclad monitors (U.S.S. *Tecumseh*, U.S.S. *Manhattan*, U.S.S. *Winnebago*, and U.S.S. *Chickasaw*) and 14 wooden ships (U.S.S. *Hartford*, U.S.S. *Metacomet*, U.S.S. *Brooklyn*, U.S.S. *Octorara*, U.S.S. *Richmond*, U.S.S. *Port Royal*, U.S.S. *Seminole*, U.S.S. *Lackawanna*, U.S.S. *Kennebec*, U.S.S. *Monongahela*, U.S.S. *Itasca*, U.S.S. *Ossipee*, U.S.S. *Galena*, and U.S.S. *Oneida*) against a Confederate squadron of one ironclad monitor (C.S.S. *Tennessee* flying the flag of Admiral Franklin Buchanan) and three wooden ships (C.S.S. *Morgan*, C.S.S. *Gaines*, and C.S.S. *Selma*). The Confederate ships were lying right under the guns of Fort Morgan on the eastern side of

The Battle of Mobile Bay in a view from the north toward the open sea, with Fort Morgan on the left. The Federal fleet was commanded by Rear Admiral David Farragut. The force entered the harbor on August 5, 1864. The Federal fleet moved in two lines, with its four ironclad monitors between the Confederate guns and Farragut's 14 wooden ships.

Opposite Top:
Farragut and his
officers on the bridge
of the U.S.S. *Hartford*
in the Battle of Mobile
Bay.
Opposite Bottom: The
view from Fort Morgan
looking north into
Mobile Bay.

**David Glasgow
Farragut**

For further references
see pages
7, *9,* 80, *110*

The son of the
celebrated General
Zachary Taylor,
Lieutenant General
Richard Taylor
commanded the Army
of Tennessee before
its final posting into
the Carolinas. He then
returned to the
command of the
Department of Eastern
Louisiana,
Mississippi, and
Alabama, and
surrendered his
command in May 1865.

the entrance to Mobile Bay. The western
side was protected by Fort Gaines on
Dauphin Island, and the entrance was
also protected by shoals, obstructions,
and mines (known as torpedoes in the
terminology of the day). Fort Gaines was
also under siege by part of the 5,500-man
detachment of Major General Gordon
Granger's XIII corps made available by
the Department of the Gulf.

Farragut's ships stood in past the
punishing fire of the forts and the enfilading fire of the *Tennessee* as they passed
Fort Morgan into Mobile Bay, and the
Tecumseh was sunk by a mine. A steady
barrage of gunfire and rammings seemed
not to affect the *Tennessee*, which was
pounded into surrender only after a lucky
shot had carried away one of her steering
chains. The Federal forces then took the
forts (Fort Morgan surrendered on August
23) and, as they were in control of the

entrance to Mobile Bay, effectively sealed
off the Confederacy's last major port in
the Gulf of Mexico after the U.S. Army had
failed to achieve this task. The Battle of
Mobile Bay cost Farragut 319 casualties
out of 3,000 men, while the Confederates
lost 312 casualties out of 470 naval
personnel involved.

Sherman's Plan of Strategic Genius

Farther to the north, however, Sherman
was still only halfway through his great
wheeling movement from the western
theater into the rear of the Army of
Northern Virginia. Like Grant in the east,
Sherman now appreciated the virtual
impossibility of trapping his opponent,
especially in so large an operational area.
Early in September 1864, he used

The Battle of Cedar Creek on October 19, 1864, was the last major engagement of Sheridan's Shenandoah Valley campaign. Reinforced to a strength of 18,400 men, Jubal Early devised a bold and ambitious plan to move stealthily through the Massanutten Mountains to hit the rear and left wing of the Federal forces as they devastated the valley. Sheridan, believing the campaign all but over, was absent in Washington and had left Major General Horatio Gouverneur Wright in command. The Confederate VIII and XIX Corps fell on the wholly unprepared Federal VIII Corps, which fled in panic. The rest of the Federal army checked the Confederates in three positions, but seemed on the verge of defeat just before the arrival of Sheridan. The Federal commander rallied his men and drove Early all the way back to New Market. Of the 30,830 Federal soldiers involved, 5,665 became casualties, while of the 18,410 Confederates, 2,910 were killed or wounded. Yet the battle finally broke Confederate resistance in the valley.

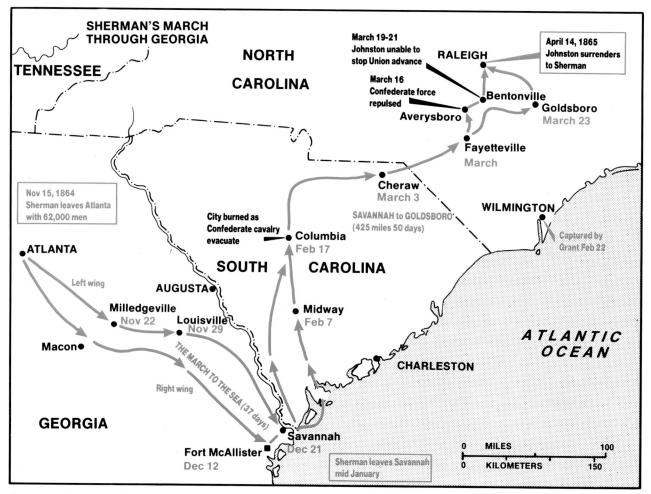

SHERMAN'S MARCH
THROUGH GEORGIA

TENNESSEE

NORTH

CAROLINA

March 19-21
Johnston unable to
stop Union advance

RALEIGH

April 14, 1865
Johnston surrenders
to Sherman

March 16
Confederate force
repulsed

Bentonville

Goldsboro
March 23

Averysboro

Fayetteville
March

Nov 15, 1864
Sherman leaves Atlanta
with 62,000 men

Cheraw
March 3

WILMINGTON

SAVANNAH to GOLDSBORO
(425 miles 50 days)

City burned as
Confederate cavalry
evacuate

ATLANTA

Columbia
Feb 17

Captured by
Grant Feb 22

SOUTH

CAROLINA

Left wing

Milledgeville
Nov 22

AUGUSTA

Louisville
Nov 29

Midway
Feb 7

ATLANTIC
OCEAN

Macon

THE MARCH TO THE SEA (37 days)

Right wing

CHARLESTON

GEORGIA

Savannah
Dec 21

0   MILES   100

Fort McAllister
Dec 12

Sherman leaves Savannah
mid January

0   KILOMETERS   150

the excellent Federal telegraph system to outline a pair of complementary strategic moves to Lincoln and Grant. Sherman's suggestion envisaged the defense of Nashville and Tennessee against any northward Confederate move by Thomas's Army of the Cumberland, reinforced by two of Sherman's corps (30,000 men in all) and bolstered as required by locally recruited formations. He himself would then take four corps totaling 62,000 men in all. Severing all connection with his lines of communication, he would live off the land as he marched through Georgia to the sea in an advance that would destroy the Confederacy's will as well as its ability to sustain the war by laying waste to every farm, railroad, and storage facility he encountered. Sherman was confident that he could reach and take Savannah (or alternatively Pensacola or Charleston), where he could then link up with the U.S. Navy and be resupplied. Meigs expressed

his approval of the scheme without serious reservation. Lincoln and Grant were less enthusiastic, but ultimately gave Sherman their permission as a show of confidence.

Sherman was first determined to make sure that Atlanta was of no further use to the Confederacy, so selected buildings were burned and all railroads in the area were destroyed.

Sherman's march to the sea began on November 12, 1864. Sherman's men had rations for 20 days and, heading for Savannah, lost all contact with Grant as soon as they left Atlanta. With no Confederate force to check its advance, Sherman's men advanced in a column four corps and 60 miles wide, burning or otherwise destroying everything that they did not need. Sherman's force arrived outside Savannah on December 10, and once the Confederates had evacuated this important port on December 21, Sherman was able to occupy it as an

Sherman's "march to the sea" through Georgia, and then his progress through the Carolinas in the closing months of the Civil War.

1864 Christmas present for the Union. The Confederacy was now divided into three parts. Already sundered into two parts when Grant's triumph at Vicksburg split off the portion west of the Mississippi River, the Confederacy had now been fragmented even more as Sherman's crushing progress split the eastern heartlands into northeastern and southwestern sections.

Already lying off the harbor to resupply the Federal forces was a fleet of supply ships. Only after he reached Savannah and regained contact with Grant did Sherman learn of the final outcome of events in his rear.

Hood Strikes Back

Sherman had been involved in the start of these events after the capture of Atlanta.

As a first step after his loss of this city, Hood had sidestepped the Federal advance guard at Jonesboro by shifting west from Lovejoy's Station to Palmetto. Here the Army of Tennessee was refitted as much as Confederate resources would permit, and President Jefferson Davis arrived on a visit designed to bolster Confederate morale after the defeat of Atlanta, and to plan a new strategy with Hood. The initial scheme envisaged continued movement west into Alabama, where Hood could receive supplies up the Blue Mountain and Selma Railroad as far north as Jacksonville. Tennessee, and then an advance toward Chattanooga. The threat to Chattanooga and then possibly to Nashville would, Davis and Hood hoped, force Sherman to fall back from Atlanta.

Sherman was indeed worried about his communications, which began to look

The waterfront in Savannah, Georgia. The marshes in the background were impassable, so an amphibious descent on Savannah was virtually impossible.

increasingly threatened once the cavalry corps of Forrest (8,000 men) and Wheeler (2,000 men) moved into central Tennessee during early September and began a campaign against Federal depots and communications in that area. Sherman felt that, where Forrest raided, Hood might then advance. Toward the end of the month, he detached one division for the protection of Chattanooga, and another to hold Rome, which shielded the Georgia Central Railroad between Chattanooga and Atlanta. Grant was also worried by the growing threat to Sherman's communications, and he urged Sherman to deal with Forrest once and for all. At the end of the month, Sherman responded by sending another division back to Chattanooga. He also posted Thomas to Nashville to improve local defenses and put all detached garrison forces on the alert.

The Confederate strategy seemed to be working, for Sherman had apparently started to dissipate his forces. Sherman however, had no intention of weakening himself so much that his plan against Savannah might become impossible.

On September 29, Hood crossed the Chattahoochee River with 40,000 men and two days later was on the move northward through western Georgia. Even though the overall Confederate strategy was clear to Sherman, the Federal commander found it difficult to

Left: A few Gatling guns were used toward the end of the Civil War. It was in essence a machine gun with an external power source (a hand-turned crank) and ammunition fed from an overhead hopper.

Below: Federal heavy artillery at Fort Totten, near Rock Creek Church, Washington, DC, in April 1865. Throughout the Civil War, the defense of Washington was an overriding concern of the Federal authorities.

locate Hood precisely, for his Confederate counterpart moved swiftly and shielded his progress effectively.

On October 3, Sherman was confident enough of Hood's approximate position to leave Slocum's XX Corps as garrison at Atlanta while he pursued Hood with 55,000 men. The campaign now mirrored that of the summer as Sherman advanced on Atlanta without being able to engage Hood in open battle. The Confederate commander pushed north to Chattanooga with his Federal adversary roughly paralleling his route, but farther to the east and without any real chance of pinning Hood. At Cross Roads, just south of Chattanooga, Hood finally felt that he had drawn Sherman into the position at which he might test the Federal army in battle.

However, Hood's subordinates agreed that Confederate morale was too low for a pitched battle, and Hood reluctantly fell away to the west in the direction of Decatur, Alabama. At this point, Sherman finally received word that Grant was about to give permission for Sherman's planned drive on Savannah. Even so, Sherman saw the destruction of Hood as essential.

Hood felt that he was now in danger of having to face the concentrated forces of Thomas and Sherman. He decided that his best course of action was a quick advance to the north, where he might tackle and defeat Thomas before Sherman could intervene. Hood then planned to move into Kentucky and Tennessee to strengthen his army in a concentrated recruiting drive. This move offered the

possibility of tackling Sherman, if the Federal commander decided to follow him into Kentucky. Then, he could push east through the Cumberland Gap to link up with Lee. Beauregard had commanded all Confederate troops in the west since September 28, and on October 21, he signaled his approval of Hood's overall plan.

Lack of Confederate Speed is Decisive

Speed was of the essence to Hood's plan, but his timetable was thrown out by alterations made to his disposition plan by Beauregard. Perceiving the threat to Nashville, Sherman reinforced Thomas with Stanley's IV Corps on October 26 and with Schofield's XXIII Corps on October 30. He also ordered Major General Andrew Jackson Smith's corps to break off its campaign against Major General Sterling Price's Confederate force in Missouri and move to Nashville.

On November 2, Sherman received word of Grant's permission for the Savannah campaign, and by November 10, Sherman's forces were on their way back to Atlanta.

Hood was slowly building a force of 39,000 men at Florence, Alabama. Thomas was building to a strength of 28,000 in Nashville, and Schofield had placed his 34,000-man corps at Columbia, Tennessee, on the Duck River and on Hood's probable line of advance. Hood set out on November 19 with his army deployed in three columns. Each consisted of one infantry corps, to link up with Forrest's cavalry corps that was already in touch with Schofield on the Duck River. On November 26, Hood closed on Schofield's position at Columbia and decided to envelop it by sending two infantry and one cavalry corps around to the east before pushing north to cut the Federal line of retreat through Spring Hill. Here, on November 29, the Confederates lost an excellent chance to trap and destroy Schofield's corps, which then undertook an unopposed flank march right across the Con-

federate front to reach Franklin, Tennessee, and dig in.

The Battle of Franklin

Hood reached Franklin on November 30, and the resulting Battle of Franklin was a complete disaster for the Confederate cause. Beginning at about 3:30 p.m. and ending at nightfall, Hood threw 18,000 of his best troops into a frontal assault against determined Federal soldiers behind well-planned defenses. Hood committed 26,900 men and suffered 6,252 casualties (5,550 killed and wounded as well as 702 missing) including no fewer than 13 generals, while Schofield committed 27,940 men and suffered 2,326 casualties (1,222 killed and wounded as well as 1,104 missing). During the

The Tennessee State Capitol in Nashville under construction.

night, Schofield fell back from Franklin to link up with Thomas in Nashville.

Hood's position was now difficult. Although he retained the tactical initiative, his forces were weaker than those of Thomas and Schofield, and they were very demoralized after the disaster at Franklin. His communications were poor, while the Federal forces were entrenched around a city they had held for three years and built up into one of their two major supply depots. All Hood could do was camp just south of the city and wait, thereby losing the initiative. He lacked the strength for a siege or even an effort to storm the city, and he was aware that any effort to envelop the Federal position would invite the almost certain destruction of his own communications. Such a demoralization of his army would mean that any withdrawal

might turn into a headlong retreat and then a rout.

The Battle of Nashville: A Tactical Masterpiece

Thomas prepared to attack Hood on December 10, only to have his plans halted by an ice storm. Unhappy about the delay, the authorities in Washington seriously considered removing Thomas, but on December 15, Thomas launched the Battle of Nashville as a classic example of the coordinated attack. In the two-day battle, Thomas committed his main strength against Hood's left flank, while a simultaneous secondary attack fell on the Confederate right flank. Everything went exactly to Federal plan. While the secondary attack pinned Hood's right flank, the primary attack swept around his left flank with the aid of the reserve (Schofield's XXIII Corps and Brigadier General James Harrison Wilson's cavalry corps), which was committed at just the right moment. The Confederates managed to fall back on December 15, but Thomas repeated his attack on the following day, and the Confederates broke. Only the classic rearguard actions fought by Forrest's cavalry prevented the total destruction of Hood's army, whose remnants halted only after reaching Tupelo, Mississippi, on January 10, 1865.

Thomas committed 49,775 men and suffered 3,061 casualties (387 killed, 2,562 wounded, and 112 missing). Hood, on the other hand, committed only 23,210 men and suffered an unknown but comparatively small number of killed and wounded, perhaps 1,500 in all, as well as 4,462 missing. It was the end of the Army of Tennessee. Hood was removed, and his army was broken up to reinforce more effective fighting forces. The Battle of Nashville had therefore removed one of the Confederacy's two remaining major armies, leaving Lee's Army of Northern Virginia as the only significant fighting force between the Union and victory.

The Civil War Approaches Its End

The stage was now set for the closing

The Battle of Nashville on December 15-16, 1864, was a monumental defeat for the Confederacy which ended any hopes that it may have had of holding any part of this vital area. Thomas planned and executed a brilliant double envelopment that completely destroyed Hood's Army of Tennessee.

campaign of the Civil War. There were, of course, a number of smaller campaigns still in progress in many areas of the vast theater of war, but the climactic campaign was to be waged in Virginia. The scene for this dying Confederate effort was set in the north by Grant's siege of Petersburg, and in the south by Sherman's arrival in Savannah. On December 27, 1864, Grant ordered Sherman to move north from Savannah and strike through the Carolinas to join up with the Army of the Potomac along the line of the James River. On route, Sherman was to be reinforced near the Carolina Capes by Schofield's corps moving from Nashville by railroad,

river, and sea, while Meade was to continue his battering ram effort against Petersburg.

Lee, in no doubt that the end was near, wrote to Davis that the Confederacy could only gather its forces for a last-ditch stand. At this late moment, the Confederate congress in February 1865 conferred on Lee the position of supreme commander, but there was precious little left for Lee to command.

Sherman moved through Columbia, South Carolina, in February and then pressed forward to take Wilmington, North Carolina, thereby removing from Confederate control its last major

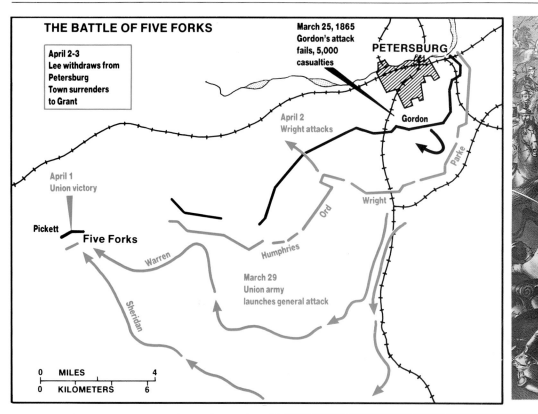

THE BATTLE OF FIVE FORKS

March 25, 1865
Gordon's attack
fails, 5,000
casualties

PETERSBURG

April 2-3
Lee withdraws from
Petersburg
Town surrenders
to Grant

Gordon

April 2
Wright attacks

Parke

April 1
Union victory

Wright

Ord

Pickett

Five Forks

Warren

Humphries

Sheridan

March 29
Union army
launches general attack

| 0 | MILES | 4 |
| 0 | KILOMETERS | 6 |

seaport. Sherman continued north, and the Confederacy reappointed Johnston to command. Johnston tried his hardest, but there was little or nothing that his shattered and badly equipped forces could achieve against Sherman's superb fighting force.

Toward the end of March, Grant and Meade renewed their effort on the 38-mile entrenched front before Petersburg. With Sheridan's cavalry and VI Corps now back under command, Grant had 101,000 infantry, 14,700 cavalry, and 9,000 guns against Lee's 46,000 infantry, 6,000 cavalry, and 5,000 guns.

Grant's intention was still to stretch out beyond Lee's right wing and envelop the Confederate forces. On March 29, the Army of the Potomac moved yet again to its left. Sheridan and his cavalry pushed out past Dinwiddie Court House to reach Burke's Station, the junction of the Southside and Danville railroads, as infantry formations tried to outflank the Confederate right at Five Forks.

Lieutenant General A.P. Hill, commander of the Confederate right wing, was not the soldier to stand on the defensive when an offensive move was possible. He therefore launched his III

Far left: The Battle of Five Forks.
Left: The Battle of Five Forks on April 1, 1865, marked the beginning of the end for the Confederate defense of Petersburg.
Below left: Supplies for the Federal army land at City Point on the Appomattox River, Virginia.

Corps against the right flank of Warren's V Corps near Five Forks. The Federal corps was initially driven back, but counterattacked and drove Hill's corps back to its trenches. Sheridan then advanced past Five Forks only to meet a combined infantry and cavalry force commanded by Pickett. Again, the Confederates drove the Federal force back in the opening phase of the battle, but then Sheridan dug in around Dinwiddie Court House and checked Pickett, who likewise entrenched instead of falling back onto Hill's position.

Sheridan was still formally commander of the Army of the Shenandoah and used his authority to take V Corps under command. Sheridan wanted Warren to fall on Pickett's rear and destroy him, but Warren moved too slowly and Pickett was able to consolidate his position. Another attempt the following day resulted in another failure to dislodge Pickett, and Sheridan removed Warren.

Grant attacked the Confederate right again on April 2, and this time forced it back to the north. The Federal forces seized the Southside Railroad, and the Confederate forces pulled back toward Petersburg. Despite the fact that

Previous Page: The burning of Richmond, Virginia, on April 3, 1865.

A Federal field hospital at City Point on the Appomattox River.

Longstreet's corps was pulled out of the defenses of Richmond in an effort to bolster the Confederate line south of Petersburg, the situation continued to deteriorate. Lee's forces were now stretched beyond breaking point between Richmond and Petersburg, and he decided that only a breakout into more open territory offered any hope of salvation. On April 3, the Confederate forces surged away to the west and the Danville Railroad. Lee's intention was to reach Danville or Lynchburg, break free of Federal pursuit, and thus remain free to link up with Johnston.

But Grant finally had Lee in the open and was determined not to be shaken off. Substantial forces followed close to

Lee's rear and left flank, while Sheridan's cavalry streamed ahead to cut off the Confederate line of retreat. In a running battle between April 2 and 6, Lee lost Ewell's corps, cut off at Sayler's Creek, and also ran out of rations. With his men straggling and deserting, Lee then learned that Sheridan's cavalry has reached Appomattox Court House, squarely on his chosen line of retreat.

Lee Surrenders at Appomattox Court House

Lee saw that the fight was over. On April 9, Lee met Grant at the McClean House in Appomattox and asked for terms.

By April 9, 1865, Lee's situation had become hopeless. He told his officers: "There is nothing left me but to go and see General Grant, and I would rather die a thousand deaths." One of Lee's officers describes the scene:

"Convulsed with passionate grief, many were the wild words which we spoke as we stood around him. Said one, 'Oh General! What will history say of the surrender of the army in the field?' He replied, 'Yes, I know they will say hard things of us. They will not understand how we were overwhelmed by numbers. But that is not the question, Colonel. The question is, is it right to surrender this army? If it is right, then I will take all the responsibility."

One of Lee's young officers tried to convince Lee to keep fighting. He proposed that the army disperse to fight a guerrilla war from the mountains of Virginia and Carolina. Lee replied:

"If I should take your advice, how many men do you suppose would get away?"
"Two-thirds of us," I answered. "We would be like rabbits and partridges in the bushes, and they could not scatter to follow us." He said: "I have not over 15,000 muskets left. Two-thirds of them divided among the States, even if all could be collected, it would be too small a force to accomplish anything. All could not be collected. Their homes have been overrun, and many would go to look after their families.

"Then, General, you and I as Christian men have no right to consider only how this would affect us. We must consider its effect on the country as a whole. Already it is demoralized by the four years of war. If I took your advice, the men would be without rations and under no control of officers. They would be compelled to rob and steal in order to live. They would become mere bands of marauders, and the enemy's cavalry would pursue them and overrun many wide sections they may never have occasion to visit. We would bring on a state of affairs it would take the country years to recover from.

"And, as for myself, you young fellows might go to bushwhacking, but the only dignified course for me would be, to go to Gen. Grant and surrender myself and take the consequences of my acts."

He paused for only a moment and then went on.

"But I can tell you one thing for your comfort. Grant will not demand an unconditional surrender. He will give us as good terms as this army has the right to demand, and I am going to meet him in the rear at 10 A.M. and surrender the army on the condition of not fighting again until exchanged."

Lee had made a noble decision. Refusing to fight a guerrilla war saved the nation great loss. Lee also correctly anticipated that Grant would yield generous surrender terms.

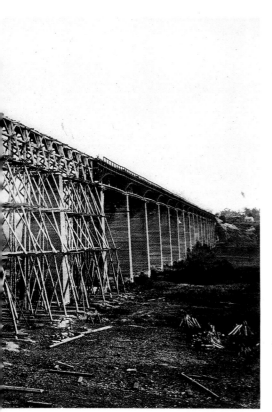

Left: The High Bridge over the Appomattox River was a landmark of the final resistance by the Army of Northern Virginia.
Below Left: The Grand Review of Federal troops in Washington, D.C., on May 23, 1865.
Below Right: Lee surrenders to Grant at Appomattox Courthouse on April 9, 1865.

Lincoln had given Grant authority to deal with Lee only on military matters, and Grant accepted Lee's surrender. As part of the terms, Grant paroled 28,356 officers and men of the Army of Northern Virginia with their horses and mules, provided rations for the Army of Northern Virginia, and forbade any of his own forces to cheer or to fire salutes for their own victory.

Johnston surrendered to Sherman on April 26, and the Civil War finally ended with the surrender of the last Confederate forces west of the Mississippi River on May 26. The dreadful Civil War was finally over. The Union had lost 138,154 men killed in battle, but the death toll was raised by another 221,374 dead from other causes, mainly disease. The overall Union death toll was 359,528. The figures for the Confederacy are less certain, but include about 94,000 killed in battle, 70,000 dead of other causes, and 30,000 dead in Federal prisoner-of-war camps. The overall Confederate death toll was about 194,000 men.

Glossary

Battalion Basic organizational and tactical subdivision of a regiment in the period before the Civil War. Generally not used in the Civil War, except in federal heavy artillery regiments retrained as infantry, which were made up of three four-company battalions, each commanded by a major.

Battery Basic organizational and tactical subdivision of an artillery regiment, corresponding to the company in an infantry regiment.

Blockade Naval operation designed to deny the enemy the use of his ports. Regular patrols try to intercept warships or merchant shipping attempting to enter or leave anywhere along the blockaded coast.

Boom Barrier across a waterway to prevent enemy movements.

Brigade Tactical grouping of two or more regiments. In the Civil War, an average brigade was made up of about five regiments. At the Battle of Chancellorsville, the Federal brigades averaged 4.7 regiments with about 2,000 men, while the Confederate brigades averaged 4.5 regiments with about 1,840 men.

Cartridge Complete round of ammunition, with the powder and projectile in a container to simplify carrying and loading.

Collier Ship designed to carry coal.

Column Body of troops with the units arranged one behind the other.

Cordon defense Area defense provided by bodies of troops strung out along the ''frontier'' of a region to detect and attack any enemy force seeking to break into the defended region.

Corps Operational grouping of two or more divisions. In the Civil War, a corps averaged about three divisions. The standard organization of the Federal corps was 45 infantry regiments and nine batteries of light artillery.

Division Operational grouping of two of more brigades. In the Civil War, a division averaged three brigades. At the Battle of Chancellorsville, the Federal divisions averaged 6,200 officers and men, while Confederate divisions averaged 8,700 officers and men.

Entrenchment Improvised defensive positions made by digging a hole or trench and mounding the excavated earth in front of the hole to provide above- ground protection.

Frigate Basic warship of the Federal navy, designed to fight other warships, but also to undertake commerce-raiding operations.

Intelligence Organization of information about the enemy's plans, movements, strengths, and dispositions.

Invest Take under siege.

Ironclad Warship protected from enemy fire by wrought iron plates (or other forms of wrought iron) over a thick wooden backing.

Judge Advocate General Officer in charge of the army's legal affairs.

Line Body of troops with units arranged one beside the other.

Line of communication Route over which men, equipment, supplies, and orders flow from a base to the formations in the front line, and over which casualties return to a base.

Maneuver battle Battle in which the commander does not seek to engage the enemy frontally, but to maneuver in a way that makes his tactical situation impossible.

Militia Bodies of troops organized on a state-by-state basis. They can be mobilized quickly under national authority in times of crisis or war.

Mobilization The process of calling citizens to arms and allocating them to the right units.

Mortar Piece of artillery designed to fire a heavy (normally explosive) projectile over a short range with a high trajectory so that the projectile plunges onto its target.

Privateer Merchant ship armed for use against the enemy's merchant shipping, and operating under the authority of a national government.

Provost Marshal General Officer in charge of the army's disciplinary affairs.

Quartermaster General Officer in charge of the army's accommodation.

Regiment Basic tactical unit in the Civil War. Federal infantry regiments contained between 845 and 1,025 men in a regimental headquarters and 10 companies lettered from A but excluding J. Each company had an authorized strength of between 64 and 82 privates, one wagoner, two musicians, eight corporals, four sergeants, one first sergeant, one second lieutenant, one first lieutenant, and one captain; real rather than establishment strengths were very much lower, and in the Battle of Chancellorsville, Federal and Confederate regiments averaged 433 and 409 men respectively.

Schooner Sailing vessel with fore-and-aft sails on two or more masts.

Squadron Detachment of warships for a specific purpose, commanded by a flag officer.

Staff Group of specialist officers who help a commander in running his unit and planning operations.

Strategy The art of planning and executing large-scale operations designed to win campaigns and wars.

Tactics The art of planning and executing smaller-scale operations designed to win battles.

Turning movement Wide-ranging movement designed to pass a body of troops around an enemy position and fall on his flank or rear.

Bibliography

Alexander, Edward P. *Military Memoirs of a Confederate.*
(Charles Scribner's Sons, New York, 1907).
A fine history by a Confederate artillerist.

Catton, Bruce. *A Stillness at Appomattox.*
(Doubleday & Co., Garden City, NY, 1953).
The second volume in Catton's Army of the Potomac trilogy.

Catton, Bruce. *Never Call Retreat.*
(Doubleday & Co., Garden City, NY, 1965).
The third volume of Catton's popular trilogy emphasising events from a northern viewpoint.

Cochran, Hamilton. *Blockade Runners of the Confederacy.*
(Greenwood Press, Westport, CT, 1973).
Expoloits of the men and ships that maintained the lifeline of the Confederacy.

Connelly, Thomas L. *Autumns of Glory – The Army of Tennessee 1982-65.*
(Louisiana State University, Baton Rouge, 1971).
Focuses on the underpublicized exploits of one of the South's two great armies.

Esposito, Vincent J. (ed.). *The West Point Atlas of American Wars 1689-1900.*
(Frederick A. Praeger, New York, 1959).
A fine map book coordinated with easy-to-understand text.

Foote, Shelby. *The Civil War: Red River to Appomattox.*
(Random House, New York, 1974).
The final volume of Foote's popular trilogy, emphasizing events from a southern viewpoint.

Hassler, Warren, Jr. *Crisis at the Crossroads.*
(University of Alabama Press, 1970).
The first day at Gettysburg.

Hoehling, Adolf A. *Last Train for Atlanta.*
(Thomas Yoseloff, New York, 1958).
Eyewitness account of 1864 in Georgia.

Johnson, Robert U. and Clarence C. Buel (ed.). *Battles and Leaders of the Civil War.*
(8 vols. The Century Co., New York, 1884-87).
A superb reference work written by the generals who led the armies.

McDonough, James Lee. *Chattanooga – A Death Grip on the Confederacy.*
(University of Tennessee Press, Knoxville, 1984).

Pullen, John J. *The Twentieth Maine.*
(J. B. Lippincott Co., Philadelphia, 1957).
An excellent unit history about the regiment which held Little Round Top.

Scott, Robert Garth. *Into the Wilderness with the Army of the Potomac.*
(Indiana University Press, Bloomington, 1985).

Memoirs of General William T. Sherman.
(Indiana University Press, Bloomington, 1957).

Sorrell, C. Moxley. *Recollections of a Confederate Staff Officer.*
(McCowatt-Mercer Press, Jackson, Miss., 1958).
Interesting characterization by one of Lee's staff officers.

Taylor, Walter H. *Four Years With General Lee*
(Bonanza Books, New York, 1962).
By Lee's Adjutant General.

Index

Page numbers in *Italics* refer
to illustration